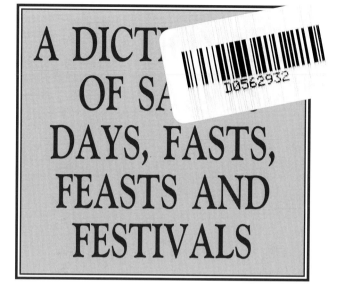

A DICT... OF SA... DAYS, FASTS, FEASTS AND FESTIVALS

COLIN WATERS

COUNTRYSIDE BOOKS
NEWBURY · BERKSHIRE

ISBN 1 85306 824 1

Produced through MRM Associates Ltd., Reading
Typeset by Techniset Typesetters, Newton-le-Willows
Printed by Woolnough Bookbinding Ltd., Irthlingborough

CONTENTS

INTRODUCTION

Local, family and general historians who must rely largely on dates to follow their interests are constantly coming up against the problem of documents or accounts that mention saints' days or other holidays without giving the actual date according to the calendar. Everything from legal documents and newspaper accounts, to private letters and diaries can present problems in this way. Without a ready-to-hand list, many hours of research may be necessary.

Hark Hark, the dogs do bark, the beggars are coming to town
Some in rags and some in bags and some in velvet gowns.

The above rhyme has been repeated throughout the ages by generations of children, but few today would realise that it has a specific reference to a once popular public holiday known as *Beggars' Day*. This took place on 11 November as part of the Feast of Martinmas and had its origins in the Middle Ages when pilgrims returning from the crusades would already be familiar with the self same nursery rhyme.

There are many fascinating facts attached to our saints' days, feasts and other festivities, many of which have been lost to memory, or at best have survived greatly changed from the form in which they were originally celebrated. Few now could recognise a saint simply from the way he or she is depicted in art, yet in days gone by, illiterate peasants would not only recognise each saint, but would associate with them a particular day in the year (often more than one day) when that particular saint had his or her festival celebrations.

It is not, however, only Christian saints who have made their mark on our social calendar. Many Pagan practices still survive, either in their original form or in Christianised feasts and festivals celebrated on the same day. For instance, the ancient Roman horse festival of *Equiria*, once celebrated by soldiers in Northern Britain involving the sacrifice of a horse and accompanied by chariot racing, archery contests etc, falls on the same day (15 October) as the Christian festival commemorating St Teresa of Avila. Though there is no evidence to link the two, it is interesting to note that this Carmelite nun is often depicted with her heart pierced by an arrow.

Who today has heard of the once commonly celebrated *Bread Festival* or of *St Dismas's Day* (the patron saint of the 'dismal', including condemned prisoners, prisoners without hope of release, the abducted and even those who organise funerals)? *Knut's Day* and *Carling Sunday* (when black peas were given free by publicans to their guests) have likewise been relegated to obscure references in archival documents and local history books.

It is interesting to see how astrological aspects are often incorporated into our modern calendars. The date of the celebration of Easter being one example, in that the date upon which it is celebrated today is still calculated using the Spring Equinox. Astronomy was also used to pin-point the days upon which other festivities should be celebrated. Few will be aware of the *Metonic Cycle* and the related *Golden Number* which are directly linked to many of our annual customs. We can only wonder if once, as in ancient Greece, the practice of remembering these dates, which are based on the phases of the moon, was by inscribing them in gold lettering on all major religious buildings.

It is only when we learn of such historical matters that we begin to see how our strange annual customs had real significance to our ancestors. Often without realising why, we continue to burn bonfires, bless boats and wells, parade through the streets in processions, dance our Morris dances and even play football matches with giant footballs, on set annual dates. We have regrettably as a nation almost lost the true purpose of why we follow these annual rituals, though it is perhaps down to some innate 'folk memory' that we continue to do so. The reasons for the loss of countless traditions are many. A number of British festivals were forbidden by Oliver Cromwell and were either carried out in secret or were abolished altogether. Many were never revived. Others re-emerged as strong as ever when Charles II, known as the Merry Monarch, came to the throne and gave his approval to the old festivities. The ravages of bubonic plague in the Middle Ages and the commencement of the First and Second World Wars are just two other examples of how history has played its part in the disappearance of these special commemorations. With their loss has also gone the ancient intrinsic importance of why we continue to celebrate the relatively few festivities that do survive in their original form.

In ancient times, documents would often be dated with relationship to a saint's day, eg, *'in octavis die Santa Alexander'*, (a week after the festival of St Alexander). On a different level, family records can be confusing when they refer only to a person dying on, say, *Collop Monday*, *Wren Day* or *Oak Apple Day*. Such holidays were once in common parlance and needed no further explanation other than the year in which they occurred. Today such references may lead to a researcher ploughing through countless reference books in an attempt to fix the exact date.

This book has been compiled as a quick reference guide to dating many special days on which celebrations or annual customs take place. Though the entries are centred around festivities in the British Isles, many of them because of cross cultural links will be just as relevant to other countries. The entries are taken from a variety of sources and have been collected over many years. Sources have included everything from individual family documents to learned encyclopaedias.

It would take many volumes to give anything other than basic facts about the large number of festivals that are and have been celebrated throughout the British Isles over the centuries. In this particular book, well known saints' days and festivities have not been expanded upon as other more substantial works can be consulted if the reader requires more information about them, eg the *Times Book of Saints*. Instead, an attempt has been made to include many of the more obscure festivals and to give whatever basic facts are known about them. A list of reference sources is given at the end of the book and in addition, a short supplementary list of date-associated words is supplied to assist in understanding old legal documents and written texts.

Names of old feasts and festivals, particularly saints' days, can be found in a variety of forms (eg Latinised, in English, or in adopted foreign language versions). Sometimes saints had more than one festival. For example, a holy day to celebrate their birth, another for their translation (moving of a body from its original place of burial to another more permanent site) and of course, the date of the death itself were often commemorated. Further confusion is found when more than one person of the same name is commemorated on either the same or different dates. Where variations occur (with or without explanations) in the sources consulted, these have been presented as found. Each entry is listed alphabetically by name together with the date generally celebrated and any supplementary information. Saints' names are listed by name only (omitting the word 'Saint' , eg *Patrick*). Those festivals described as *Eve of* usually indicate the evening before the day or date given, as often a festival ran from midnight to midnight. It should be remembered that the inclusion of a festival does not indicate that it is still in existence. Because there are six Jewish calendars, readers should consult the one for the year being investigated to find out the exact date of the Jewish fasts and festivals listed.

Festivals of the Church in Britain came into general use in the 13th century when Christianity became more formalised. However, Pagan and pre-Pagan festivals were held in just the same way, often on the same dates though some festivities were transferred to other dates or were combined with festivals already in existence.

It should always be remembered that most saints' days and festivals also changed when a new calendar was adopted and this should be taken into account when dates are found that differ from modern conventions. An example of this is the Winter Solstice and related festivals which were originally dated at 25 December but were later transferred to the 21st of that month. Similarly, Christmas has itself been celebrated on different dates depending on which calendar was in force at the time. When festivals or holidays changed in this way, some people continued to celebrate them on the old date whilst others readily adopted the new version. Others, to save confusion, or as a result of it, celebrated festivals on both the old and new dates, often giving a new name to one of them and thereby creating another festival altogether.

Despite all this, the task of pin-pointing specific dates will I hope be made much simpler with the aid of this book. Wherever possible, entries have been cross-referenced to guide you towards a deeper understanding as to how different festivities are related, often despite any obvious outward connections.

> *Has not everything in Rome, formerly heathen,*
> *now become Christian?*
> *Have not all the temples of the false gods been changed*
> *into churches of the saints?*
> *Has not the temple of Apollo been converted into the church*
> *of the Apostles?*
> *Has not the temple of Castor and Pollux been made the church*
> *of Cosme and Damien?*
> *Is not the Pantheon, formerly the temple for all the idols,*
> *now the church of the Virgin and of all the Saints?*

(Anastasius, librarian to Pope Boniface IV-
Quoted in *Fire Worship in Britain*)

Colin Waters

THE STORY OF THE BRITISH CALENDAR

The word calendar comes from two separate Latin words, *calandarium* meaning an account book and *calare* meaning 'to summon', possibly indicating that even in ancient times, day to day events such as commercial transactions and hearings were recorded using some kind of diary system. The fixing of feasts and festivals in the earliest times could only have been based upon naturally occurring events such as the phases of the moon, the rising and setting of the sun, the movements of the stars, the occurrences of high and low tides and of course the procession of the seasons. Nobody can know how mankind first began to link these events to births, deaths and annual events but at some point a jointly recognised calendar must have been adopted that could be adhered to over a wide geographical or administrative area.

Ten Months in a Year

The Romans originally had a year divided into ten months. This system put into practice at the time of Romulus began with a new moon, the months being Martius, Aprilis, Maius, Junius, Quinctilis, Sextilis, September, October, November, December. Januarius and Februarius were said to have been added at a later date by Numa, whilst the Emperors Julius Caesar and Augustus commemorated themselves by changing the months of Quinctilis and Sextilis into versions of their own names. In this Roman system, March, May, July and October had 31 days whilst the rest had 29 (except for February which had 28). Even in those days, scientists realised that a year of 355 days based on the phases of the moon did not tally with the year based on the solar cycle. In order to correct this another intercalary month, Mercedonis, was inserted after February to make up the 22 or 23 day difference.

The Variable Julian Calendar

By 46 BC the lunar and solar years were found to be out of synchronisation by 90 days. Attempts were made to rectify the situation. Julius Caesar declared that 67 days should be added to the calendar plus a *Mercecedonius* month of 23 days. The first Julian Calendar had thus been created. If Julius Caesar's calculation is difficult to comprehend today, it bears no resemblance to the difficulties caused to the Roman residents of the time. 46 BC became known to all as *The Year of Confusion.*

In desperation, a mathematician named Soisigenes was asked to draw up a new Julian calendar the following year. As 1 January was the day that the Roman consuls assumed office, he suggested that this should be the start of the new year. Based on an assumption that a solar year was actually 365¼ days, further days were added to various months and a leap year was created to make up the difference. Within a reasonable recognised margin of error, scientists of the time were satisfied that they had now found a trustworthy calendar.

The Birth of the Gregorian Calendar

By 8 BC the calendar had been found not to be as accurate as first thought: it appeared to have three days too many. Though the daily routine of ordinary folk was little affected by these three days, priests complained that the calculation of the equinoxes was misaligned. This point did not escape the authorities much later in 1582 when Pope Gregory XIII decided that the Julian calendar needed updating once more. The task of correcting the calendar fell to Aloysius Lilius who calculated that the vernal equinox had indeed fallen behind the Julian system. Ten days had to be somehow lost in order to bring the solar and lunar calendars into line.

Pope Gregory immediately declared that the troublesome ten days should be taken from the calendar and that 5 October would now become 15 October. With this the Gregorian Calendar was born. The rules to be followed henceforth were as follows:

Every year divisible by four to be a bissextile or leap year containing 366 days; every year not so divisible to consist of 365 days; and every secular year, 1600, 1800, 1900, 2000, if divisible by 400, to be a bissextile or 366 day year, but if not so divisible, to have only 365 days.

The adoption of the Gregorian calendar was not universally accepted. Different countries adopted it at various periods in history. In Britain, it was not until the time of George II that the Julian Calendar fell out of use. By 1752, the ten day error had grown to eleven days and it was felt that the British authorities should fall into line by adopting the now widely accepted Gregorian calendar. The Government declared that eleven days would be dropped from the calendar between 2 September and 14 September and that references to any date before 2 September 1752 should be referred to as *Old Style* whilst any date after 14 September 1752 would be known as *New Style*.

The change was not welcomed by the ordinary population who did not understand the scientific need for the alteration. Uneducated people failed to grasp the concept of losing eleven days from the calendar. Some refused to change their ways and quietly continued using the old calendar. Others took to the streets and rioted in various British towns and cities demanding that the Government restore their stolen eleven days. Some apparently, genuinely believed that they were now going to die eleven days earlier than they otherwise would have done under the old system.

Confusion was also caused in the recording of official dates. Prior to 1752 the legal year always began on 25 March and an adjustment had to be made to the days of the legal year in the same way as that of the calendar year.

Civil / Legal Year versus Calendar Year

The difference that existed between the civil/legal year and the calendar year, even before the change of calendar, still causes confusion to local and family historians. Dates such as '1648/49' are to be found in many records. All becomes clear, however, if one remembers that the first figure given (in this case 1648) represents the year according to the civil/legal year, whilst the latter represents the commonly accepted historical date.

Prior to the Norman Conquest the generally accepted first day of the year was Christmas Day. This was then changed to 1 January. From 25 March 1155, 25 March was declared to be the first day of the year and it was from this point that the civil/legal year became separated from the generally held calendar of the common people. From 1 January 1752, the calendars were reunited.

Other Calendars

As if the story of the British calendar is not complicated enough, there were, and are, various other valid calendars that have been accepted by the residents of Britain at various periods.

Christian Church Calendars. Though running in general concurrence with the accepted calendar of the time, many documents are dated only by saints' days or (as is often the case in Roman Catholic documents) by the deaths of martyrs. Dates are classed as BC – Before Christ, or AD – Anno Domini(cus), The Year of Our Lord, and are based on the accepted (but probably historically incorrect) date of the birth of Jesus Christ.

Jewish Calendar. Based on the lunar cycle but adjusted to the solar cycle. Leap years occur seven times in 19 years in order to keep Passover during the season of spring. Each Jewish month consists of 29 or 30 days. Dates are signified with the letters AM – Anno Mundi (The Year of the World) – and are based upon interpretation of text in the Talmud concerning the creation of the world.

Mohammedan (Islamic) Calendar. This consists of twelve months totalling 354 or 355 days, with months of 29 or 30 days. Dates are based on the *Hejir* or flight of Mahomet (16 July 622).

Hindu Calendar. Based on twelve months of 30 days each. An intercalary month is added every few years to correct the lacking five days.

French Republican Calendar. Following the French Revolution, the French people were told to follow a new calendar based on the founding of the new republic. It was introduced at midnight, 21/22 September 1793 and was reckoned from 29 September 1792. The months were named after the seasons and included a leap year called an Olympic. The calendar ceased to be used from 1 January 1806.

Chinese Calendar. Traditionally the Chinese have the oldest calendar in existence based on the lunar cycle. It is based on 29½ days from one new moon to the next, twelve of these revolutions making 354 days. Each two and a half years an intercalary month of 'Runyue' was inserted. Though modern China uses the Western calendar, Chinese communities often retained their own traditional system.

A

Ab. Jewish fast.

Abb. See under Ebba.

Abban mac us Cormaic. 16 March. Irish.

Abdon and Sennes. 30 July.

Abraxas. Associated at festivities originally with the Basilidians who were led by the Alexandrian gnostic philosopher Basilidies, but later with Christian gnostic ceremonies. Basilidies is credited with promoting the popularity of the belief in angels.

Achilles. 3 May. A constituent part of the Roman festival of Bona Dea.

Acorn Day. See under Oak Apple Day.

Adam and Eve Day. Christmas Eve.

Adamnan/Adomnan. 23 September. Irish saint who was once Abbot of Iona and chronicle writer.

Adraste. Feast day celebrated at either the new or full moon. This was the goddess to whom Queen Boadicea/Boudicca was said to sacrifice her male prisoners caught in battle.

Adrian (Abbot). 9 January.

Adrian the Martyr. 4 March.

Adrian (Hadrian) the Martyr. 8 September. Also known as Adrian Nicomedia. He was executed by Diocletian and his remains burnt. The charred remnants were taken by followers to be buried in Constantinople (Istanbul). He is depicted with an anvil and/or a sword.

Adrian Nicomedia. See under Adrian (Hadrian) the Martyr, above.

Advent Sunday. Closest Sunday to 30 November (St Andrew's Day) when the ecclesiastical year begins.

Adwyn. Ancient name for Advent.

Aed. Pagan fire deity whose feast was celebrated on 31 January/ 1 February. The name Aed means fire. Also called Dear Aed (see under that entry) and Little Aed. See also under Aiden.

Aedammair. 18 February. Irish saint.

Aedan. See under Aiden.

Aedan Foeddog. Feast day unknown. This Welsh saint, patron and founder of Llanhuadain, Pembrokeshire, Wales is often confused with Aiden (see under that entry).

Aeluric. 16 November.

Aesculapius. 1 January and 13 June. Roman festival.

Aestes. 27 June. Roman festival.

Aganolia. 9 January. Roman festival to honour Janus the two-faced god. His head had an old and a young face, each looking the opposite way. Its significance was the need to combine the past with the future and the wisdom of the old with the energy of the young. The celebration of Aganolia in January indicated a looking back to the old year with an anticipation of the new. See also Janus.

Agatha (virgin and martyr). 5 February. Born in Sicily and died as a martyr in AD 21, after being denounced as a Christian when she refused the advances of the local governor, Quintianus.

Agnes the Virgin Martyr. 21 January (also St Agnes' Night). St Agnes, the patron saint of betrothed couples, maidens and gardeners, died circa 300. She is depicted on religious icons with a lamb and with a sword in her throat. On St Agnes' Night, erroneously called St Agnes' Eve (this was 20 January), after a day of fasting, young single women would go to bed in silence, walking backwards before reciting:

Fair St Agnes play thy part and send to me my own sweetheart.
Not in his best nor worst array but in his apparel for every day.
That I tomorrow may him ken, from among all other men.

A poem by Keats called *St Agnes Eve* also refers to this tradition. Agnes was Roman by birth and, though a child, was burnt as a Christian. The fire was said to have died out and she was instead killed with a sword. She is sometimes also depicted standing on a pile of twigs or burning wood.

Agnes, Nativity of. 28 January.

Agonalia. 9 January and 11 December. Roman festival dedicated to Janus and the 'Living Sun'. See also Janus.

Agonia/Agonium. 11 December. Roman festival of games of combat and the sacrificing of slaves dedicated to Janus.

Aidan. 31 August. Northern Celtic saint who was Bishop of Lindisfarne. He was of Irish/Scottish extraction and became a monk on the island of Hii (Iona) before moving to Lindisfarne. Having ruled as bishop for 16 years, he became sick and died on 31 August 651. See also under Aed.

Ailbe. 12 September. Irish saint.

Alan. 27 November. Celtic saint of Brittany celebrated throughout Britain.

Alar. 1 December. A Celtic saint who was credited with protecting horses. He is also a patron saint of smiths of all kinds.

Alban. 17 or 22 June. Alban, the 'protomartyr of Britain', was put to death 22 June 303 (or 305 according to some sources) during the persecution by the Roman leader Diocletian, for sheltering a Christian priest. As a knight, he is said to have brought Masons Guilds to Britain and to have obtained the king's permission for a General Assembly. After his beheading, a church was built upon the site at 'Holy Well Hill'. This was superseded by the Abbey Church of St Alban on the same site. His body was said to have been translated to Ely during the Viking invasions. In later years both churches claimed that they had the original remains, though this is largely irrelevant as both sets of bones were destroyed by Henry VIII.

Alban Arthuan. 21 December.

Alban Eiler (Light of Earth). 25 March.

Alban Elfred. 21 September (Autumn Equinox).

Alban Elued. 21 September (Autumn Equinox).

Alban Hefin. 21 June (Summer Solstice).

Alban Heruin. 21 June (Summer Solstice).

Aldhelm. 25 May.

Alexander. 3 May.

All Fools' Day. See under Fools Holy Day.

All Hallows/All Saints. 1 November.

All Saints' Day. 1 November.

All Souls' Day. 2 November. Said to have been Christianised from a Pagan festival by St Odilo.

Allhallowe'en. Eve of 1 November.

Almacius. 1 January. Eastern monk who died circa 351 in the Roman arena when he tried to stop the entertainment because it was a Christian feast day. He was also known as Telemachus.

Alor. 25 October. Celtic patron saint of Tremeoc. Though a saint of Brittany, like all Celtic saints his feast day was celebrated throughout Britain.

Alphege. 19 April. His full name was Alphege of Aelfheah and he was born circa 954 in southern England. He took holy orders at a young age and was made Bishop of Winchester in 984. He made peace with the invading Norwegians and became Archbishop of Canterbury in 1005. He returned from Rome to find the Vikings were once more ransacking England and he was eventually captured by them in 1011. Refusing to be ransomed, he was 'pelted with ox bones and hornes until he fell to the ground' before being killed.

Alphege, Ordination of. 16 November.

Alphege, Translation of. 8 June.

Altar of Peace (Dedication). 30 January. Part of the Roman Fornacalia festival.

Amalthea. 1 May. Roman festival involving the presentation of dog statues at shrines.

Amand. 6 February. Born 584, he became a 'roving bishop' in 629 and set up various male and female monasteries.

Amatory Mass. See under Wakes.

Ambarvalia. 29 May. Roman.

Ambrose. 4 April. Ambrose (340-397) was chosen as Bishop of Milan, much to his reluctance. So much so that he had to be baptised to take up the position a week before his official election to office (7 December 374) aged 37. He was a peaceable man, and excommunicated Emperor Theodosius for organising a massacre at Thessalonica. Whilst dying on Good Friday, 4 April 397, he heard his deacons whispering about his successor. One mentioned the name of Simplicianus. Ambrose came out of his coma to say strongly, 'An old man, but a good man'. He then took Communion and died.

Ambrose (Bishop. Father of Latins). 7 December. Bishop Ambrose died in 397. He is the patron saint of beekeepers and domestic animals. He is usually depicted with a beehive, a scourge and a book.

Ananius of Damascus. 25 January. Celebrated also as the *Feast of the Conversion of St Paul* (25 January) as it was Ananius who baptised him.

Anastasius. 27 April.

Andrew. 30 November. The apostle Andrew is usually depicted with a fishing net and of course with an X-shaped cross. He is the patron saint of Scotland as well as of fishermen and sailors. Historically he is said to have come from Bethsaida in Galilee and was the brother of Simon Peter. He was martyred at Patrae and his body was later supposed to be translated to Constantinople by St Regulus under the orders of Constantine. However, the bones were instead taken to Scotland by St Regulus in defiance of Constantine and with the assistance of 'King Hung'. Hung has been identified as King Angus MacFergus, the person traditionally credited with the founding of St Andrew's in Scotland.

Angela Merici. 31 May. Angela founded the Ursuline Order.

Angerona. 31 December. Roman festival.

Angus. 11 March. Irish saint also called Oengus Ceile De and Aonghus.

Anianus. 17 November.

Anna Perenna. 15 March. Special day during the Roman Feriae Marti.

Anne. 26 July. This St Anne is recognised as the mother of the Virgin Mary and is shown in religious icons as a virgin with a child in her lap. She is the patron saint of housewives and miners and of Canada. Her husband was Joachim. Many miracles were attributed to her in the Middle Ages and though she was widely revered throughout this period, her official festival day was not declared until 1584. See also under Joachim.

Annis. See under Carling Sunday.

Annu. See under Danu.

Annunciation. 25 March (7 April in Old Style calendar). The date when the archangel Gabriel is said to have announced the forthcoming birth of Christ to the Virgin Mary.

Anselm (Bishop). 21 April. Archishop of Canterbury, usually featured in his bishop's robes with a ship which he often holds in miniature in his right hand. He was born at Aosta in 1033 and expressed an early interest in becoming a monk. He eventually became first Prior and then Abbot of Bec Abbey, and Archbishop of Canterbury in 1093. He attended William the

Conqueror on his death bed. His influence among kings was great and he gave advice to the sovereigns of England, Ireland, Scotland and Jerusalem. He died 21 April 1109 and was buried in Canterbury Cathedral before being moved to a chapel there, bearing his name.

St Anselm, 1033–1109 – Archbishop of Canterbury.

Anskar. 3 February. Scandinavian saint.

Anthony/Antony (Abbot). 17 January. Bishop Anthony is usually illustrated with a T-shaped staff or T-shaped walking stick, and carries a bell. He was born of well-to-do Egyptian Christian parents who died young and left him much wealth. Anthony gave it all away and became a religious hermit. He is said to have lived in a subterranean cavern for 30 years, existing on only bread, salt and water. He later returned to the outside world and became a preacher to crowds of pilgrims who lived together in the desert in colonies of tents. Because of this he is said to have founded monasticism. He died in 356 at the age of 105. The disease erysipelas, characterised by reddened patches of skin, is also called St Anthony's Fire.

Antonius. 2 September.

Antony. 26 December. Cornish saint who may be a Christianised version of Tan the fire deity.

Antony of Padua. 13 June. Born in Portugal, he is the patron saint of the illiterate and the poor. Also of Portugal.

Aodhan of Fern. 31 January. Irish saint.

Aonghus. 11 March. Irish saint also called Angus and Oengus Ceile De.

April Fools' Day. 1 April. See also under Fools' Holy Day and Gosling Day.

Apollinaris the Martyr & Timothy. 23 July.

Apollo. 6-13 July. Roman festival of Apollo.

Archangel(s). 29 September.

Armel. See under Athmael.

April Fools' Day – As this old print shows, April Fools' Day was as popular with children in past years as it is today.

Armilustrium. 19 October. Roman festival dedicated to Mars.

Armistice Day. 11 November. Modern festival commemorating the dead of the First World War. Celebrated with two minutes' silence at the eleventh hour of the eleventh day of November (the eleventh month). See also Remembrance Day.

Arnulf. 18 July.

Artemis. See under Diana.

Arthur, Light of. 21 December.

Athmael. 21 December. The fact that his festival coincides with that of the Light of Arthur festivity may add weight to the belief of some that King Arthur of mythology was the same person as the 7th century St Arthmael. Arthmael is a Celtic saint who was revered in Wales, the South and Brittany. He was also known as St Armel.

Arzhel. 16 August. Celtic saint of Brittany who was celebrated throughout the Celtic world.

Arzhur. 6 October. Celtic saint of Brittany celebrated throughout Britain.

Asaph. Date of festival uncertain. Welsh saint.

Ascension (of Christ). Second Thursday before Whitsuntide, known also as Holy Thursday. It is associated across the British Isles with various water festivals ranging from Well Dressing at Tissington in Derbyshire to the Planting of the 'Penny Hedge' or 'Horngarth' in the harbour at Whitby, Yorkshire. It is also the day in some areas where adults and children travel in procession to 'beat the bounds' of their parish or town, often with long sticks of willow. See also under Godric (of Finchale).

Ash Wednesday. The first day of Lent when it was traditional to mark the sign of the cross with holy (blessed) ashes (obtained from burning the palm crosses used at the previous Palm Sunday celebrations) on the foreheads of those attending church.

Assumption (of Christ). Second Thursday before Whitsuntide. Also called Ascension and Holy Thursday.

Assumption of the Virgin Mary. See under Virgin Mary.

Athanasius. 2 May. Lived c.296-373 and became Bishop of Alexandria, of which he was a native. He organised the Christian church in Abyssinia (Ethiopia). He lived a turbulent religious life, being exiled on a number of occasions and at one

Ascension – The strange 'Penny Hedge' or 'Horngarth' ceremony at Whitby (circa 1922). The ritual dates back to medieval times. Its origins are lost in antiquity but it is still carried out on the Eve of Ascension each year.

point living alone in the desert as a hermit before returning in 363 to Alexandria where he died.

Athene's Day. 4 December.

Aubyn. 1 March.

Audrey. See under Ethelreda.

August fast. 23 August.

Augustine (Archbishop). 26 or 28 May. Like Ambrose, Augustine is titled 'Father of the Latin Church'. He is the patron saint of all theologians and is usually depicted with a book and a burning or broken heart. A story tells how he came to Britain to convert the population to Christianity only to find that many of them were already Christians. Despite this, Augustine settled

St Augustine – Meeting Ethelbert, King of Kent as he (Augustine) arrived on the British mainland.

in Canterbury and assisted with the further conversion of the remaining pagans. A memorial to commemorate St Augustine's landing in Britain was erected at Ebbsfleet.

Augustine, Translation of.
13 September.

Augustine of Hippo. 28 August. Patron saint of theological students. He was born in 345 at Tagaste in Numidia. After a wild youth he joined the Manicheans, experimenting with Platoism and a number of odd beliefs. In 387 he was baptised into the Christian faith and became a priest at Hippo in 391. He wrote voluminously with strong conviction, particularly about his belief in pre-destiny which was adopted by the Calvinist movement. In Britain, Pelagius (also known as Morgan), a Welshman, continually disputed his religious beliefs. Augustine died on 28 August 430.

St Augustine – Cross erected at Ebbsfleet to commemorate his landing in Britain.

Augustinus Magnus (Bishop). 28 August.

Augustinus Magnus, Translation of. 11 October.

Augustus. 5 February. Also known as Pater Patria. Roman festival celebrating Augustus receiving the Pater Patria.

Austell. 28 June. Cornish Celtic saint.

Austine. A variation of Augustine. See under that entry.

Autumn Equinox. 21 September (equal length day and night – date variable depending on location).

Aventi. See under Ewenny.

Azenor. 7 December. Female Celtic saint of Brittany and elsewhere.

Aziliz. 22 November. Female Celtic saint.

B

Baal. Ancient deity whose festival later became the lighting of Bale Fires (see under that entry). The festival was traditionally held at the end of the rainy season or winter. The associated goddesses of Baal worship were Ashereth, Ashteroth and Anath who in turn were associated with the sun, moon and stars. Baalic temples had as a centre-point (not necessarily geographically) a stone pillar, said to mark the point where earth energies flowed from below, together with a wooden pole. The stone pillar was of a phallic nature whilst the moveable wooden pole represented Ashteroth, Baal's wife. Some believe that churches were built upon the sites of Baalic temples and that the phallic pillars were removed and replaced by 'bluestones', whilst Ashteroth's pole became the village maypole.

Bacchanalia. Celebrated at or about the Spring Equinox in Britain. In Rome it ran from 16 to 17 March. A Roman festival where drunken abandonment was allowed as a means of social engineering. It was thought that such 'outlets' at various intervals throughout the year prevented disruption and law-breaking throughout the rest of the year. Bacchus, the god of wine, was also known as Dionysus. Liberalia was also the same or another abandoned festival celebrated on the same day.

Bacchus. See under Bacchanalia.

Badarn. See under Padarn.

Baglan. Festival date unknown. Celtic.

Baisakhi. Hindu and Sikh celebration of the first day of the New Year. The festival lasts three days and is celebrated by religious readings, hymns and often processions of sword carriers.

Baithene. 10 June. St Baithene was a close relative of St Columba who was believed to have been given the task of carrying on Columba's work after his death. Scholars disagree whether he was Columba's son, stepson, brother or cousin.

Baldred. Feast day unknown. Celtic saint and writer.

Bale Fire Day. One of four days throughout the year (generally the solstices and equinoxes) when celebratory fires were lit throughout the country. A remnant of the worship of the god Baal. See also under Baal.

Bannockburn Day. 24 June. Celebrated by Scotsmen to commemorate Robert Bruce winning independence for Scotland by driving out the English at the Battle of Bannockburn.

Baptism of the Lord. Originally celebrated 6 January, then 25 December. Now celebrated on the Sunday following 6 January.

Barbara (Virgin Martyr). 4 December. She is the patron saint of firework manufacturers and of builders and in France the patron of miners and gunners. She died in 235 and is often depicted with a tower, a chalice, a sword and the altar wafer in her hand. She appears not to have been considered as a saint until the 7th century. Legend tells how she was beheaded by her own father who imprisoned her in a tower. He was then struck down by lightning. An old legend says that if branches of any flowering tree are cut on St Barbara's Day they will bloom at Christmas if kept in water.

St Barbara.

Barnabas. 11 June. Barnabas is said to have given up all his possessions to the apostles to raise funds for the Christian movement. He took the name Barnabas on beginning his religious work, his real name being Joses or Joseph. Joseph was a Levite from Cyprus. He travelled with St Paul carrying out missionary work. Though not one of the twelve apostles he is considered by some to be the '13th apostle'. A number of Epistles are attributed to him, though the assumption is believed false.

Barr(i). 27 September. Welsh saint. Possibly the same as St Barr (or Finbarr) whose festival was celebrated around the same time of the year in Ireland and Scotland. See also under Finbarr.

St Barnabas.

St Bartholomew's Day – Showing celebrations at a fair on 24 August 1721, possibly in London.

Bartholomew. 24 August. Developed from the Pagan feast of Nemesia. The saint's day is celebrated by a wide range of belief systems, and it gave his name to the St Bartholomew's Day Massacre when in 1572, 3,000 Huguenots were slain on the orders of Catherine de Medici. Historically he is associated with Nathaneal, as recorded by St John, and was said to be of noble birth. His martyrdom occurred in India where he was flogged to death.

Bartholomew of Farne. 24 June. Born at Whitby, Yorkshire to Scandinavian settlers. His name was originally Tostig but he changed it to William and later fled to Norway where he became a priest. In c.1144 he was back in Durham serving his time as a novice monk and was said to have many visions. Taking these as a sign of his religious future, he became a hermit on the Farne Islands for over 40 years. He was by now known as Bartholomew. He died in 1193 having carved his own coffin, to which the devout later came, claiming miracles caused by Bartholomew's power.

Basil. 14 June. Known sometimes as Basil the Great. He was born into a wealthy family in 329. His sister Macrina persuaded him to be baptised as a Christian around the age of 30 and he immediately set about a tour of solitary monks whom he organised into communities. He became Bishop of Cesarea in 370 and died nine years later, worn out from the religious and political struggles of the time.

Batilda. 30 June.

Battle of Britain Day. 15 September. Commemorates the Royal Air Force's victory in the air battle over Britain in the Second World War (1940).

Beal-tine (Beltain). 1 May.

Bearchan. 6 April. Celtic.

Beatrice. 29 June.

Bec(can). Easter Sunday. Celtic.

Bede, The Venerable. 27 May. Theologian(673-735) noted for his historical and religious written work. A legend relates that he was so venerable that when old and blind he preached to a pile of stones, thinking they were his congregation. So moving were his words that the stones spoke to him, saying 'Amen, Venerable Bede, Amen'. He is known as 'The Father of English History' having written *The Ecclesiastical History of the English Nation*.

Bees. 17 November. Originally a nun (for 30 or more years) at Hackness, near Scarborough, she saw a vision at the time of the death of St Hilda (related by Bede). She was later canonised as St Bees.

Bega. Feast day unknown. 15th century saint.

Beggars' Day. 11 November. Part of the Feast of Martinmas (see under Martin) when children would dress up as beggars and would go from house to house begging treats and singing:

Hark Hark, the dogs do bark, the beggars are coming to town
Some in rags and some in bags and some in velvet gowns.

The practice may have developed from the custom of giving alms to pilgrims or 'Palmers' returning from the crusades, as the same song is also known to be associated with them.

B(e)acan. 26 May. Irish Celtic.

Beha(n). See under Beryan.

Beheading of John the Baptist. See under John the Baptist.

Bel(lenus). Ancient sun/fire god (or goddess) whose feast was celebrated on Beltane (see below). She is sometimes described as the wife of Wade (possibly Woden or Thor) who is mentioned in *Leland's Itinerary* as being buried (according to local legend) close to Mulgrave Castle, Lythe, Yorkshire. A nearby village, Sandsend, was anciently called *Thordissa* and has near it a valley called *Marsdale* where a temple to Mars is said to have stood.

Bellona. 3 June. Roman festival.

Beltane. 1 May. Pagan pivotal point of the unstable spiritual world, one of the *Four Great Fire Festivals* (see under that entry also). It was the second most important after Samhain. Records of the 10th century describe May fires being lit in honour of the god *Bel* and cattle being driven through the smoke to prevent disease. In later times in Scotland and northern England, May Day was still celebrated by jumping through fires or over trenches filled with burning materials. See also Bel(lenus) above.

Benedict Abbot (Benedictines). 21 March. Founder of the Benedictine religious order. Born 480, he is the patron saint of schoolboys and of coppersmiths and is usually depicted as a Benedictine abbot with a broken tray, chalice or cup. Benedict was of noble Roman birth and became a hermit monk at the age of 14. He founded the Benedictine Order when about 50 years of age, at Monte Cassino monastery. He died in 543 and was buried beside his sister, St Scholastica. He is the patron saint of cavers and was known fully as Benedict of Subiaco.

Benedict (Abbot), Translation of. 11 July.

Benedict Biscop. 12 February. The name Biscop by which he is known means bishop. He was born c.628 and died 12 January 690, though his festival is celebrated on 12 February. Benedict was of noble birth, served under King Oswy of Northumbria and as a monk travelled to Rome where he became Abbot of St Peter's. He returned to Northumbria and under the patronage of King Egfrith founded monasteries at Wearmouth, where he was Abbot, and at Jarrow. He was teacher of the Venerable Bede and made regular journeys to Rome throughout his life.

Benedict (Bishop, Abbot). 4 January.

Benedict (Pope). 7 May. Benedict was Pope between 684 and 686. He is remembered for his support of Wilfred of York against the King of Northumbria.

Berach. 15 February. Irish saint who is patron saint of the O'Hanley clan.

Berched. 1 February. Female Celtic saint. Also called Breched.

Berchta. Wife of Woden. See under Woden and Berchta.

Bergant. Another name for St Bridget (see under that entry).

Bergwin. 26 August.

Berin. See under Berinus.

Bernard (of Clairvaux). 20 August. Founder of the Cistercian Order who died 1153. He is usually depicted as a monk in a white habit adoring the Virgin Mary or with a beehive. He is the patron saint of beekepeers and is associated with fountains. He was born 1091, the son of a knight from Burgundy and was notable for supporting Pope Innocent II against Anacletus II. He promoted the second Crusade in 1146.

Bernard (of Clonfert). Date of festival unknown. Scottish 6th century Celtic saint.

St Bernard of Clairvaux – Depicted in the white robes which were typical of the Cistercian Order.

Bernardino of Feltres. 28 September. Born at Venice in 1439. His name was Martin Tomitani but when he joined the Franciscan Order he took a name close to that of Bernardino of Sienna. He was involved with giving loans at low rates of interest and so became a patron saint of bankers.

Bernard(ino) of Siena. 20 May. Born at Massa near Sienna in 1380 and died in Aquila in 1444. He is patron saint of all in advertising and public relations and of public speakers.

Bernardine. 20 May. Little celebrated in England except at places with Franciscan connections. St Bernardine was Vicar General of the Franciscans in 1438.

Bernice. See under Veronica.

Bertin. 5 September.

Beryan. 4 June. Female Celtic saint. Also called Buryan in Cornwall and Beya(n) or Beha(n) in Scotland and Ireland.

Beth(og). 30 October. Prioress of the community on Iona.

Bird Day. 25 March.

Beya(n). See under Beryan.

Birin/Birinus. 3 December. Birinus is believed to have been born in Lombardy but in 633 he sailed to Britain, with the approval of Pope Honorius in order to preach the gospel. Landing in the region of Southampton he went to Churn Knob near Wallingford where he began his mission. He is also connected with Berins Hill, Ipsden and Bapsey Meadow, Taplow, and of course with Dorchester where he established his base. He died 3 December 649. Later when the West Saxons moved their bishopric to Winchester, Birinus's bones were translated there.

Birthday of the Blessed Virgin. 8 September, later 15 August.

Black Annis. See under Carling Sunday.

Black Crom's Day. First Sunday after Lammas. Pagan festival which was Christianised in Ireland to commemorate St Patrick's destruction of all of the pagan idols dedicated to Black Crom. Black Crom was believed to have been a phallic fertility figure.

Blaise (Blasius, Bishop and Martyr). 3 February. Patron of the strangely diverse group of woolcombers, candle makers and people with sore throats. In some countries a 'blessing of throats' still takes place during the festivities. This bishop of Sebaste died in 316 when both he and his children were beheaded. See also under Oimelc.

Blane. 11 November. Scottish saint.

Blasius. See under Blaise.

Bleddian. Feast day unknown. The name survives in the Welsh place-name, Llanbleddian.

Blood Days. The days leading up to the Vernal Equinox when the legendary Attis was resurrected after having been slain by a wild boar. Kybele (or Cybele), his lover, was said to have believed that his spirit had been absorbed by a pine tree. The tree was bound with linen strips and flowers and laid in a tomb of stone before eventually being resurrected at the Vernal Equinox. During the days leading up to the Equinox, celebrants of the festival of Hillaria are said to have worked themselves into a frenzy, cutting themselves with blades. Hence the name 'Blood Days' (Pagan). See also under Hillaria, Cybele (and Attis).

Blowing of Trumpets Day. See under Cybele.

Bogman Race Day. Easter Monday. Held annually at Great Finborough, Suffolk and dates back to at least 1897 when teams of ploughmen fought for a ploughing contract. It was decided that the contract would be thrown in the air and the first team to get it over the threshold of the local pub would win the right to work. The prize today is free beer. It is thought that the race is an adaptation of traditional ploughing festivals which date back much further than 1897.

Bona. 29 May. Born in Pisa, Italy c.1156. She died peacefully in 1207 having lived a life of pilgrimages and failing in her attempt to convert the Saracens to Christianity. She was once the female patron saint of travellers and is now considered the patron of air hostesses.

Bona Dea. 3-4 May. Roman festival beginning at dusk on 3 May and ending at dawn the following day. A single day festival of the same name was held 3 December.

Bonfire Day. See Midsummer Bonfire Day.

Bonfire Night. See Papist Conspiracy.

Boniface. 5 June. Bishop and martyr, Boniface is the patron saint of both brewers and tailors, and of Germany. He is depicted by the image of an axe in the root of a tree. He is celebrated by both Anglicans and Roman Catholics. Historically he was born in Crediton, Devon of wealthy parents, c.680 and died in 755. His original name was Wilnfred, but he adopted the name Boniface when he became a monk and missionary. He travelled extensively, eventually becoming Archbishop of Mainz where as papal legate he had jurisdiction over the German tribes. He never returned to England. Having resigned his powerful position in 754 to preach the gospel to the heathen Fresians, he met his end. He was attacked and killed at Whitsuntide when attempting to carry out confirmations of previous baptisms. The bloodstained copy of a book called *The Advantage of Death* with which he tried to protect his head during the attack, was preserved as a relic in the monastery at Fulda which he had earlier founded.

Botulf/Botolph 17 June.

Boxing Day. 26 December. The English Folk Dance Society founded by Cecil Sharp was said to be inspired by Sharp witnessing a 19th century traditional Boxing Day dance being performed in an Oxfordshire village. The dance with strange steps, accompanied by a man with a concertina, is said to have fascinated Sharp and led to him codifying many other traditional dances that would otherwise have been lost. At other villages such as Marshfield in the Cotswolds, mummers would set out dressed in strange costumes to perform mummer plays. Boxing Day is said to takes its name from the tradition of servants being given Christmas boxes containing gifts on this day. Their employers also allowed them the day off to celebrate after waiting on the family on Christmas Day (ie, it was the servants' Christmas Day celebration). It was once traditional for pantomimes to begin on Boxing Day and to run for two months.

Branding Sunday. First Sunday in Lent (also called Firebrand Sunday, Spark Sunday and Brandon Sunday).

Brandon Sunday. See under Branding Sunday.

Brandubh. 6 February or March. Celtic.

Branwalather. 9 February. Cornish Celtic saint.

Breaca. 4 June. Female Cornish Celtic saint.

Bread Festival. 1 August.

Breched. 1 February. Female Celtic saint. Also called Berched.

Brede. 1 February. Isle of Man.

Bre(a)nden/Breannain/Brendon 16 May. Irish/Scottish saint. Celebrated in Brittany as St Brendan the Navigator. See also under Malo.

Breoc. 1 May. Cornish Celtic saint.

Brevalaer (Bishop). 19 January. Saint of Brittany widely celebrated throughout Celtic Britain.

Briac. 22 December. Celtic saint from Brittany who was commemorated throughout the Celtic world.

Brice. 13 November. Roman Catholic saint who died in 444. In Britain his name is remembered via the Massacre of St Brice's Day of 1002 when Ethelred ordered the killing of all Danes in England. He is also known as Britius. Historically he is known to have served under St Martin at his monastery in Tours; Martin had possibly brought him up from a child as he was said to have caused his parents much trouble. This troublesome aspect of his character was evident in the adult and he became an unpopular bishop. He was accused of immorality and left his position for some years before returning to continue his ministry for another seven years. He died in 444.

Bridal. Also known as Bride Ale. In early times it was used as the name for any festival or celebration, but later came to mean a nuptial feast for a wedding.

Bride. 1 February. Scotland. See also under Bridget.

Bride Ale. See under Bridal.

Bridgit/Bridget of Kildare. 1 February. Abbess Bridgit or Bridget died in 625 and is the patron saint of cattle and dairymaids and of all fugitives. Her emblem is a lighted lamp, lantern or flame. She is the patron saint of all nuns in Ireland and of farm and dairy workers. She had various names including Bergant and Brigantia. See also under Brighid.

Briec/Brieg. 1 May. Saint of Brittany widely celebrated throughout Celtic Britain.

Brigantia. 1 February. Another name for St Bridget (see under that entry).

Brighid. 1 February (Pagan pivotal period of instability of the material world). A Pagan saint whose name is also spelt Brigid, Brig, Bridget etc.

Britius (Bishop). See under Brice.

Bruno. 6 October. Founded the Carthusian Order. Born c.1030 and died 1101.

Buddha. See under Wesak.

Burning of the Clavie. 31 December and previously on New Year's Eve in the old calendar. Barrel burning ceremony which still takes place in various places in Scotland. The clavie is a barrel and the ceremony is always in the charge of the 'skipper' indicating a link to burning boat ceremonies.

Burns Night. 25 January. Celebrated in Scotland and throughout the world where Scots gather in memory of their national poet, Robert (Rabbie) Burns.

Buryan. See under Beryan.

Buthek. 8 December. Cornish Celtic saint.

C

Cadell. Feast day unknown. Welsh. Also known as Cadle.

Cadfan. 1 November. Welsh saint.

Cadle. See under Cadell.

Cadoc. 24 January. Celtic saint whose feast day was widely celebrated thoughout Britain and Brittany. Also known in Brittany as Kado.

Cadwaladr/Cadwaller. 9 October. Welsh saint.

Caelfind. 3 February. Irish saint.

Caesarius of Arles. Feast day unknown. Caesarius (470-543) was instrumental in eradicating Pagan practices and pressed for the penalty of excommunication for all those who took part in them.

Caileech. See under Carling Sunday.

Cainnech. 11 October. Irish saint. Also known as Kenneth and possibly (in Wales) as Cennech.

Cairbre (Bishop). 3 May. Irish. St Cairbre was Bishop of Moville.

Cairbre. 1 November. Irish. This St Cairbre was Bishop of Assaroe.

Caireach. 9 February. Female Irish saint.

Cairell of Tir Ros. 13 June. Irish.

Caemgen. 3 June. Irish Celtic saint, also called Caoimhin.

Calixtus. 14 October.

Callisto. 12 February. Roman one day festival that fell within the longer festivals of Fornacalia and Concordia.

Calnneach. 11 October. Scottish saint, also called Coinneach.

Calum. 9 June. Scottish saint.

Camps, Feast of. 2 November.

Candlemas. 1 February (Candlemas Eve) and 2 February (Candlemas Day). See also Lupercalia and Oimelc from which it evolved. In Roman times it was known as Hypapante, meaning 'Meeting' and celebrated the meeting of Jesus with Simon and Anna in the Temple (as described in the Bible in the second chapter of Luke's Gospel).

Canute. 19 January. Scandinavian saint who was also King of England. Known for the incident when it is said he tried to halt the tide by his command. In reality he 'commanded' the tide in order to show that his powers were no greater than that of a normal man. He was son of Sweyn 'Forkbeard' who drove Ethelred the Unready out of Britain in 1013. Sweyn was accepted as king by the English Witan and on his death, his place was taken by Canute. He died at Shaftsbury on 12 November 1035 and was buried in Winchester, having united all his dominions in peace. His name is sometimes spelt Knut. In Sweden they burn the Christmas tree on his holy day.

Caoimhe. 2 November. Irish.

Caoimhin. 3 June. Irish Celtic saint also called Caemgen.

Caput Jejunii. Latin for 'the head of the fast' (ie the first day of Lent).

Cara Cognatio. See under Caristia (below).

Carantoc. 16 May. Cornish Celtic saint.

Carbry. 3 May. Isle of Man Celtic saint.

Caristia. 22 February. A Roman festival at which all family quarrels were traditionally forgotten. Also known as Cara Cognatio.

Carling Sunday. Fifth Sunday in Lent or the second Sunday before Easter Day. The word Carling (or Carle, Carline, Care etc) means 'Maid' and the celebration involved whirling dances (hence Whirling Sunday). Carling Sunday was a northern festival celebrated until the 1960s, when black carling peas, boiled and served in vinegar, were eaten and were given away in local public houses. The word Cailleach is believed to be a Celtic transliteration of Kali (meaning black). Kali or Kali Ma (black mother) was the Hindu wife of Siva. She is associated with the dark side of the moon and all evil. In the East, men were sacrificed to the goddess by being impaled on hooks from which they were whirled around until death. In Scotland 'car cakes' were eaten. In many societies and languages the last sheaf of corn cut was called the 'old woman' or 'old wife' (in Scotland it was also called 'Cailleach' meaning 'the Black Maid') and was dressed as an old woman. There was intense rivalry to cut the first 'old wife' before any neighbours. In Antrim a corn dolly was made from part of the last corn sheaf and was called a 'Carley'. Reapers would throw sickles at it and the one who cut it in half was allowed to take it home. In Scotland it is said that a cult existed to worship Kali and it has been speculated that they were called the Kaledonio, hence Caledonia (ref: *Gogmagog* – Lethbridge p 162). There is a strong resemblance here to the festival of Black Anni(s), once celebrated (at least in Leicestershire) as Cat Anna and widely as Catana. The Monday following Carling Sunday was commonly known by the coarse title of 'Farting Monday' in reference to the great number of black peas eaten.

Carmentalia. 11 to 15 January. Roman festival dedicated to Carmen(ta).

Carna. 1 June. Roman festival.

Carneval. An old name for Lent (see under that entry).

Casimir. 4 March. Saint celebrated by Eastern churches. He is the patron saint of Poland and Lithuania.

Castor and Pollux. 20 May. Zodiacal Roman festival dedicated to the 'Heavenly twins' (Gemini).

Catan/Cat Anna. Moveable Easter feast day (Celtic) with possibly the same origins as Carling Sunday (see under that entry).

Catherine of Sienna. 29 or 30 April. Patron saint of Italy. She was born at Sienna and was said to be one of 25 children. At age 16 she was taken into the Dominican Order as a 'mantellatae sister' and as such wore the nun's habit but lived at home. Later she corresponded with many great leaders. In 1378 she went to Rome, working under the leadership of Pope Urban VI and died there on 29 April 1380. She was canonised by Pope Pius II in 1461.

Catherine (Virgin Martyr). 22 or 25 November. She died in 310 and is often depicted strapped to a wheel. Her emblems are a book and a wheel. She is the patron saint of wise men, philosophers and mechanics as well as being patron of all spinsters. She is known as Catherine of Alexandria to distinguish her from Catherine of Siena. Her martyrdom is said to have come about when she was executed after trying to convert the Emperor Maximus to Christianity. Though associated with the wheel as the mode of her martyrdom, the wheel is said to have miraculously broken before or at the time of her execution and she was in fact beheaded. Her head, in legend, was taken to Mount Sinai by angels. Her day was for centuries one of the best celebrated throughout Europe

following her being brought to the notice of common people by
the Crusaders. Up to the end of the 1800s, her festival, known
as Cattarn's Day was celebrated by lacemakers, especially in
Lincolnshire, Northamptonshire and Bedfordshire where a
special cake and ale was made and children walked in
procession, dressed in white, led by 'the Queen' wearing a
crown and holding a sceptre. The name Cattarn appears to
have been a common pronunciation for Catherine as Catherine
of Aragon was called Cattarn la Fidele in a popular song of the
time. Cattarn became corrupted to 'cat and' and Fidele became
'fiddle' and was represented as the Cat and the Fiddle in the
children's nursery rhyme and on inn signs (according to a
footnote in the book *Catherine of Aragon* by Francesca
Claremont, p99). See also under Katherine.

Ceadda. See under Chad.

Ceallachan. 22 April. Irish saint.

Cecilia (Virgin Martyr). 22 November. This 2nd or 3rd century
saint is the patron saint of musicians and is generally pictured
with a musical instrument, especially an organ or violin. There
is little known about her though her feast day was being
celebrated as early as 394 at a Roman church dedicated in her
name and where her bones were believed to be buried. She is
said to have been married to a young man called Valerian but
told her husband that her viginity was being protected by an
angel until he agreed to convert to Christianity. This he did. St
Cecilia's Chapel in Rome is built upon the site of the Roman
bath in which she was drowned during the Christian persecutions there. Pope Paschal I translated her relics with great
musical ceremony in 817 and it is possibly for this reason that
she is always shown with at least one musical instrument in
religious art.

Cedd(e). 7 January. Sometimes confused with Chad, his brother.
Cedd was Bishop of the East Saxons at London. Of Northumbrian birth, he founded Lastingham Abbey and acted as
interpreter at the Synod of Whitby. He died at Lastingham in
665.

Cennech. Little-documented Celtic saint. Possibly the same as St
Kenneth (St Cainech). See under Cainnech.

Ceolfrith(i). 25 September.

Cera. 9 September. Irish saint known fully as Cera of Killahear.

Cerealia. 19 April. Continuation of the Pagan festival of Ceres. During Cerealia the Romans celebrated the potential harvest of the coming 'six vegetative months'.

Ceres. 1-19 April, 1 July, 24 August, 23 September, 1-5 October, 18 November and 3 December. Festivals in honour of the Roman goddess of agriculture. At least some of these feast days were celebrated by all Pagan societies. Ceres is the Roman equivalent of the Greek goddess Demeter. There was also a single day named the Festival of Ceres which fell on 2 February and was part of the Fornacalia festivities in Roman Britain. It continued with celebrations called Ceralia (see under that entry).

Ceres – As depicted on a statue in the Vatican, Rome.

Cernunnos. May festivities. Antler God who was anciently celebrated during the de-horning of cattle and also deer. Hill figures such as the Cerne Giant are also associated with his festivities.

Cetsamhain. 1 May.

Chad. 2 March. Also called Ceadda. He was one of four brothers who were all clergymen, one of whom was St Cedd who Chad succeeded as Abbot of Lastingham. Chad was consecrated Bishop of York but stood down on the return of Wilfred from France, allowing him to become bishop. He later became Bishop of the Mercians at Lichfield. He died 2 March 672.

Chair of St Peter. 22 February.

Chalceia. See under Samhain.

Chanukah/Chanucah. See under Hanukkah.

Charles (King). See under King Charles.

Childermas. 28 December. Commemorating Herod's murder of the innocent children in Bethlehem. Also known as Holy Innocents' Day. Once believed to be the most unlucky day of the year and the reason for the postponement of the coronation of Edward IV until the following day.

Chinese New Year (Lantern Festival). See under Teng Chieh.

Chiron. 3 May. A constituent part of the Roman festival of Bona Dea.

Christ, Presentation in the Temple. 2 February.

Christ the King See under Christus Rex.

Christina. 24 July.

Christingle. Moveable church festival for children where they are given an orange (symbolising the world) wrapped in a red ribbon (symbolising Christ's blood). The orange is pierced with four cocktail sticks (symbolising the four seasons – or elements?) upon which are pierced pieces of fruit, or fruit flavoured jelly sweets (symbolising the fruits of the earth). In the centre of the top of the orange is placed a lighted candle (symbolising Christ as

Christ's Presentation at the Temple – celebrated in the Old Style calendar on 15 February and in modern times on 2 February.

the light of the world). The church service accompanying the ceremony is usually held in the weeks leading up to Christmas. Some sources give its origins in the Moravian church during a Christmas service in 1747 at Marienborn Castle, Germany, by Bishop Johannes von Waterville though others say it stretches back in time to a commemoration of St Lucy, who is sometimes confused with St Lucia. Lucy was martyred in Scandinavia and has her saint's day commemorated on 13 December. See also under Lucy.

Christmas Day. 25 December(formerly in the Old Style calendar, 6 January). An old northern tradition is that it was in Yorkshire that the first English Christmas Day was celebrated, when in York in 521 King Alfred of the Danes having killed 90,000 of his enemy, settled in for the winter period. While there he rebuilt all the churches that had been burned to the ground and ruled that only Christian ceremonies should be performed in them. It was traditional up until the commencement of the First World War in 1914 that grocers would give boxes of Christmas candles to their regular customers symbolising, it is said, the star that led the three wise men to Bethlehem. The first person to enter a house on Christmas Day was known as the 'lucky bird' and was said to bring good luck to both themselves and the household they were entering. See also under Epiphany.

Christmas – An 1874 illustration entitled 'Preparing for Christmas' and showing a family using a dog to pull home a Christmas tree.

Christmas Eve. 24 December (5 January by Old Style calendar). See under Epiphany.

Christmas, Old. 6 January. See under Epiphany.

Christmas Vigil. See under Easter Vigil.

Christopher. 25 July. The well known patron saint of travellers and sailors who is always depicted with Christ as a child on his shoulder. The origin of people wearing a St Christopher medallion was not only to protect them during travelling but also to protect the wearer from dying, as it was said that anyone who saw the image of St Christopher would not die on the same day. Historically he was martyred as a Christian during the persecutions around 250. He is said to have been descended from the Canaanites and was of great stature, being twelve cubits tall.

St Christopher – Featured on a Victorian prayer card.

Christopher (martyrdom). 28 March.

Christus Rex. Last Sunday in the year, also called the Day of Christ the King. Also the last Sunday before 11 November.

Chrysogonus. 24 November.

Ciar of Kilkeary. 5 January and 16 October. Irish.

Ciaran. 9 September. Irish saint.

Circumcision. 1 January. Commemorates the circumcision of Christ. Believed by some to be probably a Christianisation of ancient fertility practices.

Ciriacus. 8 August.

Ciricus and Julitta. 16 June.

Clare (Abbess). 12 August. Abbess Clare died in 1253 and is depicted in a brown habit with a cord belt. She carries a monstrance (a transparent or glass-faced shrine). Clare was the founder of the Order of Sisters of Poor Clare.

Clarus. See under Cleer.

Claude of Besancon (Bishop). 6 June. Patron saint of gingerbread sellers and toy makers. He died in 699 and is depicted on icons with a child at his feet and often carrying a whistle or other toy.

Claus. See under Nicholas (Saint and Bishop).

Clavee. See under Burning of the Clavee.

Clean Monday. The first Monday of Lent.

Cleer. 4 November. Also called Clarus. Gives her name to the parish of St Cleer near Liskeard.

Clement (of Rome). 23 November. 1st century saint and one of the first Bishops of Rome to be installed. Clement was supposedly ordained by St Peter himself. He may or may not be the same person as Flavius Clemens, the Roman Consul who was a relative of Domitian.

Clier. See under Cleer.

Close Sunday. See under Low Sunday.

Coemgen. See under Kevin.

Coinneach. 11 October. Scottish saint, also called Cainneach.

Colan. 21 May. Cornish Celtic saint, possibly same as the Welsh St Collen. In Cornwall the festival was also said to be celebrated on the 'Sunday after the first Thursday in May'.

Collen. 21 May. Welsh saint, possibly same as Cornish St Colan. The altered name survives in the Welsh town name of Llangollen.

Collop Monday. Monday before Shrove Tuesday. Collop Monday is a northern festival when eggs and collops (slices of dried, salted meat) were eaten. See also Shrove Monday.

Colman. 18 February (8 August in Ireland). Bishop Colman was an Irishman who became a monk on Iona, later becoming Bishop of Lindisfarne in 661. He took a major part in the Synod of Whitby where Celtic and Roman clergy argued about the future of the Christian church. After the synod, the disgruntled Colman moved to Inishbofin Island, Mayo, where he died on 8 August 676.

Colm Cille. 9 June. Irish.

Colomon. 13 October. An 11th-century Scottish-born saint who was arrested as a spy in Austria, on his way to Jerusalem, and was hanged. He became one of the patron saints of Austria.

Columba. 13 November. Female Cornish Celtic saint. See also under Columba (Abbot).

Columba (Abbot). 9 June. Scottish apostle who is often depicted carrying a basket of bread and/or the orb of the world enveloped or emitting a ray of light. Not to be confused with the female Cornish saint of the same name or St Columbanus. Historically it is known that Columba was born at Gartan, Co. Donegal on 7 December 521 and was of the O'Donnel clan. He became a monk after being educated by St Finian at Moville and was ordained c.546. He founded Irish monasteries at various places including Derry and Durrow before crossing the sea to Scotland as a missionary. He is supposed to have been permanently banned from Ireland after encouraging men to fight in the battle of Culdreimne (561). He then moved to Iona in 563 and founded a monastery there which spread its influence throughout the northern part of the British Isles. He is credited with converting the Picts to Christianity and died at Iona on 9 June 597. See also under Oran.

St Columba – 521–597.

Columbanus. 24 November. Born in 543 in West Leinster, Ireland of noble parents who sent him to a Bangor university to be educated. In 583 he moved to Burgundy where he stayed for two decades, founding a number of monasteries. His name is perpetuated in the Lombardy town of San Columban. Later he fled from Burgundy to Germany and Switzerland, finally arriving in Italy in 612, and died at the monastery he had founded in Bobio. The writings of Columbanus were published in 1667 at Louvaine.

Comgan. 3 or 5 March. Celtic. Irish royal uncle of St Fillan.

Comhghall. 10 May.

Commemoration of St Paul. See under Paul.

Commemoration of the Faithful Departed. The last three Fridays after Epiphany commemorate, in turn: faithfully departed priests, all faithfully departed, and those who died away from home, family and friends.

Compitalia. 1-5 January. Five-day Roman festival, the first day of which was known as the festival of Pax.

Compitalia (of Lares). 12 January. Roman.

Conan of Man. 26 January. Celtic saint commemorated on the Isle of Man and elsewhere.

Concord. 11 June. Roman festival used to re-dedicate the temple of Concord.

Concordia. 16 January. Roman festival. Also 5-17 February, a longer festival which ran in conjunction with the festival of Fornacalia.

Conlaed. 3 May. Irish saint. Also spelt Conley and Conleth.

Conleth. See under Conlaed.

Conley. See under Conlaed.

Conran. 14 February. Scottish saint, possibly same as St Conval.

Consualia. 21 August. Roman festival dedicated to Consus. Also celebrated 15 December.

Conthigerni. See under Kentigern.

Conval. 14 February. Scottish saint, possibly same as St Conran.

Conversion of St Paul. 25 January. See under Ananius of Damascus.

Corentyn. 1 May. Cornish Celtic saint.

Cornelius (Pope). 16 September. He was martyred in 252 and is the patron saint of all domestic animals, particularly cattle. His emblems are a papal tiara and a bull's horn.

Cornelius and Cyprian. 14 September.

Corpus Christi. Moveable church feast generally held the Thursday after Whit Sunday. It began in the West as the festival of the Holy Eucharist in 1264.

Cosmas and Damian. 27 September.

Costentyn. 9 March. Cornish Celtic saint.

Cowan. 13 October. Celtic.

Cowel. 10 May. Celtic saint from the Isle of Man.

Crassus, Defeat of. 9 June. Roman festival commemorating the defeat of Crassus by the Parthians.

Creed. 30 November. Female Cornish Celtic saint.

Crescentia. See under Vitus.

Crimthann. 23 May. Irish. Also called Criofan.

Criofan. See under Crimthann.

Crispin(ian). 25 October. Patron saint of shoemakers, who once held a special trade holiday on St Crispin's Day. Crispin and Crispinian are recognised by the Roman Catholics as two separate brothers who were both shoemakers living in Soissons. They were beheaded as Christian martyrs in 285. The Battle of Agincourt was fought on St Crispin's Day and their names are spoken by Henry V in Shakespeare's narrative of that battle.

Crom's Day. See under Black Crom's Day.

Cronan. Feast day unknown. St Cronan was an Irish saint, known to have baptised St Kevin (see under that entry). At the moment of baptism, a legend says that four angels appeared by the font carrying tapers burning with an unusual radiance. This glow was said to have surrounded St Kevin for the first seven years of his life, which were unusually sunny.

Cross Day. 28 December. Irish version of Childermas.

Cross, Invention of. 3 May.

Cuthbeg. 31 August.

Cuthbert (Bishop). 20 March. He gives his name to *St Cuthbert's beads*, a naturally occurring bead formed from the detached fossilised stems of encrinites. He is believed to have been of Scottish birth, serving his early years as a shepherd. He became a monk at Melrose. Later he was sent to a new abbey at Ripon, but with others refused to abandon the practices of the Celtic church in favour of Roman ones. Consequently he returned to Melrose. A tale of a fish snatched from an eagle, only for it to be given half back by Cuthbert is an allegory on the split in the Christian Church (the fish) under the power of Rome (the eagle). In 676 he retired to the Farne Islands and became Bishop of Lindisfarne in 685. At Christmas 686 he predicted his own death and died two months later.

Cuthbert, Translation of. 4 September. The Abbots Bromley Horn Dance or Dance of the Deer Men was traditionally held on the first Monday after the Feast of the Translation of St Cuthbert. Twelve Staffordshire yeomen dressed in waistcoats, tight breeches, long socks and flat beret-type hats would each select a set of antlers (kept in the local church) and dance through the town to music, holding the antlers aloft.

Cybele (and Attis). 22 March (Old Style calendar). Also 4-10 April. A Roman festival celebrated throughout Europe in which a pine tree was cut down and brought into the temple to the altar of Cybele. A guild of tree bearers performed the ceremony, after which the tree was worshipped as if itself a god. (Attis was said to have been turned into a pine tree.) Its trunk was swathed with strands of coloured wool and it was decorated with violets to represent the purple blood of Attis, and roses and anemones to represent the blood of Adonis. On the following day there was a ceremony of the blowing of trumpets and on the third day known as the Day of Blood, the high priest bled himself ceremoniously as a sacrifice to the memory of Attis. The Cybele tree festival and its treatment of the tree as Attis is probably the origin of our own May Day and Maypole celebrations. See also under May Day and Cybi, below.

Cybi. Spring festival. It would seem that this Welsh saint is a Christianised version of Cybele (see above).

Cying the Neck. Festivities that once accompanied the harvesting of corn crops. It is possibly a dialect expression meaning scything the heads of corn.

Cyndeyrn. See under Kentigern.

Cynidr. Welsh saint associated with well ceremonies. Possibly the same as St Cynydd or St Cyndeyrn.

Cynog. Festival date unknown. Welsh.

Cynydd. See under Cynidr.

Cyprian. 14 September. Noted for his care of the sick, particularly sufferers of the Plague. He survived persecutions and plagues himself but was beheaded at Carthage on 14 September 258. In order that his festival did not coincide with that of the Holy Cross, his feast day was often held on 16 September or on 26 September. Some references give other dates and facts about his life, and a date of death as 282. See also Cyprian and Justina.

Cyprian and Justina. 26 September. Cyprian, Bishop of Carthage (North Africa) was considered one of the early 'Christian Fathers'. He lived c.200 to 282 and came to be bishop following a career in law. He is noted for his work against the persecuted and in providing hospitals for those with the plague and other diseases. During the Decian persecution (250) he went into hiding but in 251, 252 and 256 he presided at the synods of African bishops. During the Valerian persecutions of 257 he was exiled to Curubis (Kurba) in Tunisia but returned the following year only to be executed.

Cyril. 18 March. Cyril lived 315-386 and was Bishop of Jerusalem between 350 and 386. In 358 he was accused by the Arian bishops of selling church property to feed the poor and was expelled from the city, though he later returned. Cyril is credited with instigating the first formal system of theology.

Cywair. 15 November. Celtic saint celebrated in the ancient festival of Gower, another version of his name.

D

Dabhaid. 24 May. Scottish form of David.

Daigh of Inishkeen. 18 October. Irish saint.

Damasus. 11 December. Born Rome 304 and died 385 aged 80. Patron saint of archaeologists because he spent his life exploring and documenting Rome's catacombs.

Damhnait. 13 June. Irish saint.

Daniel. See under Deiniol.

Danu. May festival. Once celebrated in Ireland. Also called Annu.

Dasius. 20 November. Martyr who was beheaded rather than take part as the 'King of Misrule' during the Pagan, Roman Saturnalia festival. The details of his death, if accurate, are possibly the most precise of any saint. It was recorded as *'At Durostorum by the soldier Joannes on Friday 20th November being the 24th day of the moon at the fourth hour'*.

David. 24 May. Scottish saint, also called Dabhaid.

David (Archbishop). 1 March. Died 1 March c.544 (though some sources give different years as late as 601). Sometimes depicted with a dove upon his shoulder. He is the patron saint of Wales and of poets and was nicknamed 'The Waterman' as he is said to have drunk nothing else. The holiday also celebrates King Cadwaller's victory in a battle of 640. St David is said to have converted the Welsh to Christianity and is known as Dewi Sant or St Daveth in his native Wales. He is also considered a Cornish saint and in Brittany was known as St Devi. In legend he is credited with being the uncle of King Arthur and a grandson

St David – patron saint of Wales.

of King Ceredig. He is said also to have been a pupil of Paulinus. The Welsh emblem of a leek is said to have been instituted by him after a battle against the Saxons as all the Welsh wore leeks to distinguish themselves on the battlefield. Historically he is known to have been Bishop of Menevia (St David's), to have undertaken a pilgrimage to Jerusalem and to have presided over two church synods. Pope Calixus made him a saint in 1120.

Day of Absolution. An early name for Good Friday.

Day of Ashes. See under Ash Wednesday.

Day of Atonement. Jewish festival of Yom Kippur.

Day of Blood. See under Cybele.

Day of Gainsaying. Same as Day of Questions. See below.

Day of Our Lord's Passion. Good Friday.

Day of Preparation. An early name for Good Friday.

Day of Questions. Seventeenth Sunday after Pentecost also called the Day of Gainsaying, commemorating the day the Pharisees questioned Christ in the Temple.

Dea Dia. 17 May. Pagan.

Dead, Festival of the. 1 November.

Dear Aed An Irish misnomer for Dei Aed (the god of fire). Also called Little Aed. See under Aed.

December Fasts. 20 and 24 December.

Declan. 24 July. Irish.

Dedication Festival. First Sunday in October. This date is used for the dedication of churches if not on a prescribed feast day.

Dedication of Altar of Peace. 30 January. Part of the Roman Fornacalia festival.

Dedication of the Temple. Jewish celebration.

Dedication of Vica Pota. See under Vica Pota.

Deilo. See under Teilo.

Deiniol 11 September. Welsh Saint. Also called St Daniel.

Deis Cinerum. The Day of Ashes (i.e. Ash Wednesday).

Demetrios. 26 October. Celebrated by Greeks in the UK.

Deniol. 11 December. Celtic saint also called Denoel.

Denis/Denys. 9 October. Known also as St Dionysius but

celebrated on a different feast day from another saint of that name who was the companion of St Paul. St Denys is the patron saint of France and is depicted in some religious art carrying his own head in his hands. Whilst in France preaching the gospels he was said to have been put to death at Montemarte (Martyr's Mount). A story relates that after his beheading, he picked up his head and walked with it to the site of St Denys' Abbey. He gave his name to the French kings' battle cry '*Mon Joie St Denys*'. See also under Dionysius.

Denoel. 11 December. Celtic saint also called Deniol.

Denys. See Denis.

Derrien. 7 February. Saint of Brittany widely celebrated throughout Celtic Britain.

Devi. See under David (Archbishop).

Devote. 27 January.

Dewi Sant. See under David (Archbishop).

Diana. 13 August. She was also known in Greece as Artemis. In Roman times a festival dedicated to Diana lasted from 26 to 31 May as well as 13 to 15 August and was characterised by games dedicated to Prosperine. Her son was Hippolytus who was dragged to his death by horses. See also under Hippolytus.

Diana – Above: She is illustrated in the traditional classical way. Right: She appears in a totally different form as the many breasted figure of Artemis, found at Ephesus in Turkey, where the Temple of Diana/ Artemis was included among the seven ancient wonders of the world. The Artemis cult stretches back further to the cult of Cybele, mother goddess of Anatolia.

Dies mandati. See under Maundy Thursday.

Dionysus. 25th December. See under Bacchanalia and Denis.

Dippy Day/Dipping Day. Cornish version of May Day when everyone wore a sprig of may (hawthorn). Those that did not would have water thrown over them by revellers. Also known as 'Dipping Day' in the same county when on the first Sunday in May revellers would bathe in the sea and could customarily throw anyone into the water who was fully clothed if they were not wearing a sprig of may blossom.

Dismas. 25 March. Patron saint of the 'dismal'. Included in this category are condemned prisoners, prisoners without hope of release, the abducted and interestingly those who organise funerals. St Dismas's nickname is 'The good thief'.

Distaff Day. See under Rock Day.

Divalia. 31 December. Roman festival. See also Festival of Light(s).

Dochau. Festival day unknown. Welsh.

Dog Days. 3 July-15 August. These dates are generally accepted as variable as they are based on the 'heliacal rising' of the Dog Star which from ancient times was considered to bring the hottest and most unwholesome days of the year in the northern hemisphere when dogs were liable to go mad.

Dominic. 4 August. Founder of the Dominican Order whose emblems are a black and white dog carrying a torch in its mouth, a star and a lily. Early worshippers celebrated 5 August. He was born 1170 in the Castilian area of Spain and was educated at Palencia university. At 25 years of age he became a canon at Osma and visited Languedoc during the Albigensian Heresy period where he formulated the rules for his new Order. At Venice in 1221 he became very sick and travelled to Bologna where he died on 6 August 1221.

Dominic, Translation of. 19 or 24 May.

Dominica in Albis Deponendis. See under Low Sunday.

Domnach Crom Dubh. See under Black Crom's Day.

Donan. 16 April, also 25 September. Died as a monk on the island of Eigg, Scotland at Easter 618. Donan was also revered in Brittany and widely throughout Celtic Britain.

Donat. 7 August.

Donatian. 15 October.

Donnan. 17 April. Scottish saint.

Dorothy (Virgin Martyr). 6 February and 19 May. Died c.300. She is usually depicted with the Christ child at her feet and carrying a basket of fruit and flowers. She is the patron saint of gardeners and of brides.

Dunmow Flitch. Ceremony held, traditionally in June or July at Dunmow, Essex, when a flitch of bacon was given to any couple who could prove they had not argued in the past year. The ceremony appears to have its origins at Little Dunmow priory and may be a commuted service from monastic times.

Dunstan (Bishop). 19 May. Bishop Dunstan was born c.924 and died 988. He was connected by blood to the Wessex royalty and his family had estates near Glastonbury Abbey where he was educated. He was also related to Bishop Alphege of Winchester who eventually persuaded him to take religious vows, though he was originally determined to marry. This proposed wife is believed to be the maiden used

St Dunstan – This Victorian cartoon illustrates the legend that Dunstan was tempted by the Devil, but defeated him by grabbing his nose with a pair of tongs.

by the devil to tempt him, which is often spoken of in accounts of his life. He is depicted in religious art holding a pair of goldsmiths' tongs (often nipping the devil's nose) together with a host of angels. He is the patron saint of goldsmiths, blacksmiths and blind people and was a goldsmith by trade.

Dunstan, Ordination of. 21 October.

Dunstan, Translation of. 7 September.

Dwywe. Unknown feast day. Welsh.

Dwyn. 25 January. One of the few female Welsh saints.

Dyfan. Feast day unknown. Welsh.

Dyfrydwy. Welsh water goddess festival. Her name survives in the Welsh place-name Glyndyfrydwy, meaning Dyfrydw's Glen.

Dympna. 15 May. She is the patron saint of the insane. A legend tells us that she was the daughter of an Irish chieftain and a secret Christian who escaped to Belgium where she miraculously was able to cure the insane. In 1850 the establishment in Gheel, where she was said to have worked, was made into a formal mental hospital. In religious icons she is depicted fighting with a devil.

E

Eadburga. 15 June.

Eanswith. 31 August.

Easter Day. First Sunday after first full moon after the vernal equinox, a date decided at the Synod of Whitby in 664 in a verbal battle between the Celtic and Roman church representatives over (among other things) which church calendar should be universally observed. That of the Roman church was adopted causing a split within certain factions of the Celtic church.

Easter Even. See under Holy Saturday.

Easter New Fires. Celtic Christianisation of Pagan fire festivals at Easter time.

Easter Octave. The eight days starting from Easter Sunday. The last day being called Quasimodo Sunday from the Latin entrance song *Quasi modo geniti infantes* (Like new born babes).

Easter Vigil. Easter vigil which dates back at least to Roman times and now takes place on the Saturday during Holy Week. It is celebrated by the use of a wax candle which is inscribed with the cross. The letters alpha and omega are inscribed at the top and bottom and the four numbers representing the current year are inscribed from left to right above and below the cross arms. Five grains of incense representing the wounds of

Easter – A sheet torn from an unknown publication of the 1820s shows that 'lifting' was a common part of the Easter celebrations at that time.

Christ are sometimes pushed into the soft wax. Other vigils are held (in the Roman rite) at Christmas and Pentecost. Many such 'night watches' used to be held on various saints' days in the past.

Ebba. Festival date variable. She was also known as St Abb. An Anglo-Saxon princess, she was shipwrecked with two sisters in Northumbria at St Abb's where a monastery was built.

Edana. 9 January. Female Scottish saint.

Edern. 26 August. Saint of Brittany widely celebrated throughout Celtic Britain.

Edith. 16 September (See also under Osyth)

Edmund (Archbishop). 16 November. Born at Abingdon to Christian parents around 1170. He studied theology in Oxford and Paris and is known for his treatise *Speculum Ecclesiae*. He became Treasurer of Salisbury Cathedral in 1222 and preached in favour of a Crusade. After three previous elections to the Archbishopric of Canterbury being quashed, he was eventually elected as Archbishop in 1233. Throughout his life he fought many political as well as religious battles and died at Soissy on 10 November 1240.

Edmund (Archbishop), Translation of. 9 June.

Edmund (King and Martyr). 20 November. He is usually depicted as a bearded king with an arrow in his hand. He was a Kentish clan leader (841-870) who was appointed by Offa, King of the East Angles, to be his successor. He was wrecked off the coast of Norfolk at a place now known as St Edmund's Point whilst travelling for his coronation, which was evidently delayed until later. He fought against the Danes but lost the battle and refused to accept the defeat unless his overlord would become a Christian. The Danish Prince Hingmar refused and tied Edmund to a tree where he was whipped and had arrows shot at him. He died there at Hoxne. Though his body was discarded, it was eventually collected by an allegorical 'grey wolf' and was buried at a place where a small chapel was erected which grew into the monastery of Bury St Edmunds.

Edmund (King and Martyr), Translation of. 26 April.

Edward (King and Martyr). 18 March. The boy king (c.963-978) succeeded to the throne when only twelve years old. On a visit to his step-brother Ethelred who lived at Corfe Castle, he was met by residents of the castle who gave him a cup of wine to drink. As he partook of the wine he was stabbed in the back and was then buried without ceremony in a rough grave. Dunstan later organised a great ceremony for the translation of his body and he was re-interred in a tomb at Shaftesbury.

Edward (King and Martyr), First Translation of. 18 February.

Edward (King and Martyr), Second Translation of. 20 June.

Edward (King and Martyr), Trial of. 20 June.

Edward the Confessor. 5 January. Classed as a saint, King Edward (1004-1066) is depicted either holding or giving a ring (to a pilgrim) and before St George was adopted, was the patron saint of England. Son of Ethelred the Unready and Emma of Normandy, he was King of Wessex and the last Saxon king of England. Though he was educated at Ely he lived most of his life in Normandy until he was crowned king in 1042. There appears no agreed reason by scholars why he was sainted, or indeed why he was called 'the Confessor'. His greatest claim to religious fame is that he built Westminster Abbey.

Edward the Confessor, Translation of. 13 October.

Edwin. 12 October. A former prince of Deira (Yorkshire), he was baptised a Christian in 627, possibly at York where a church that he built eventually owned his head as a religious relic. His body is said to be buried at Whitby Abbey where his daughter Enfleda and granddaughter Elfleda became abbesses.

Efflam. 7 November. Saint of Brittany widely celebrated throughout Celtic Britain.

Egg Day. 13 April.

Egidius. 1 September. He was also known as St Giles (see under that entry).

Egwin. 30 December. A 7th century Bishop of Worcester.

Egyptian Day. Applied to any Friday, especially Good Friday, believed to be very unlucky.

Eid-Ul-Fitr. Part of the Islamic festival of Ramadan (see under that entry). This festival begins on the 29th day of the month, ending the fast. However, if no moon is seen on that day, then an extra fast must be kept.

Eighan. See under Kevin.

Eimhin. 22 December. Irish saint.

Eithon's Day. The date of the celebration of this once widely held

Pagan festival is now lost. The name of the goddess survives in the Welsh place-name, Blaeneithon, meaning 'source of the Eithon River'.

Elevation of Life Giving Cross. 23 September (formerly 27 September in the Old Style calendar).

Eli. Welsh saint who is little documented. Possibly same as St Eligius or St Ellen.

Eligius. 25 June. Also known as Bishop Eloi or Loi. Many celebrated his feast day on 25 June though there does seem to be a substantial amount of variation regarding dates. He died in 639 and as the patron saint of all metal workers and smiths, he is depicted with a hammer and an anvil in religious icons. Also celebrated as St Giles or St Gilles (see under Giles).

Elizabeth (of Hungary). 19 November. Hungarian princess who was betrothed at 15 years of age to the eldest son of the Landgrave of Thuringia and married in 1220. In 1227 her husband died on the Crusades and she then devoted her life to caring for the sick including lepers. She died 1229 aged only 24. Her feast day was celebrated often in Britain after the Crusades but lapsed almost completely in later years.

Elizabeth I (Queen). 7 September. A feast day to celebrate the Queen's birthday. See also Eunurchus.

Ellen. Celtic saint. Possibly same as St Helen.

Elmo. See under Erasmus.

Eloi (Bishop). See under Elgius.

Elusinia (Elusian Rites). 23 September to 1 October. Pagan.

Ember Days. Days set apart for fasting and prayer in each of the four seasons of the year, being: the Wednesday, Friday and Saturday after the 1st Sunday in Lent; the Feast of Whitsuntide; September 14th; and December 13th. The weeks in which they fall are called Ember Weeks. The word ember is derived from the Anglo-Saxon *ymbren* meaning a circuit.

Emerentiana. 23 January.

Empire Day. 24 May.

Endelyon. 29 April. Female Cornish Celtic saint.

Enna. See under Kevin.

Enora. 14 October. Celtic.

Enurchus (Bishop). 7 September.

Eochaid. 17 April. Saint and Abbot of Lismore. Irish.

Eochaid (Bishop of Tallaght). 28 January. Irish.

Eoghan. 23 April. Irish saint.

Eostra/Eostra's Day. 25 March. See under Ostara.

Ephphatha Sunday. The eleventh Sunday of Pentecost. It uses an Aramaic word meaning 'be opened'.

Epiphany. 6 January (19 January in the Old Style calendar). The word means 'manifestation' and is a complex collection of a number of Christian celebrations including the arrival of the three kings at Bethlehem, the baptism of Christ in the river Jordan by John the Baptist, the water into wine miracle at Cana and the birth of Christ himself. The period is also called 'Old Christmas' and 'The Three Kings'. See also under Christmas. In some villages it was the tradition on the Monday after Epiphany (particularly in Yorkshire and Lincolnshire) for local plough boys and men to take part in 'Plough Monday' ceremonies involving parading a plough around the village accompanied by morris dancers or sword dancers. These sword dancing ceremonies still take place in country areas and have often migrated from the traditional day of celebration to be included in all country festivals. In North Yorkshire the sword dancers are still known as 'Plough Stots' even though the plough is now hardly ever included in the celebrations. See also Plough Monday and Stephen Protomartyr (also celebrated the first or second Sunday after 2 January).

Epona. Spring Equinox celebrations. British version of Hipa, the Greek goddess. A horse goddess whose festivities revolved around horse racing (and eating). The traditional Easter horse races of modern times are a remnant of her festival.

Epulum Jovis. 13 November. Roman feast day.

Equinox. See under Spring Equinox and Autumn Equinox.

Equiria. 14 March and/or? 27 February. Roman. This may have been a moveable festival as there are also records of it being held on 15 October. In the last instance it is recorded that there were chariot races and archery contests and that the 'October Horse' was sacrificed at the altar of Mars in the temple. The celebration on 14 March was the main day of a month dedicated to Mars (Feriae Marti).

Erasmus. 2 June. He was the patron saint of sailors who knew him as St Elmo. St Elmo's fire, an electrical phenomenon that

Plough Monday/Epiphany – Rare old photographs taken c.1920 of (above) sword dancers, and (below) Plough Stots, celebrating Plough Monday at the village of Goathland in North Yorkshire.

emitted a glow around the tops of ships' masts during a storm, was taken as a sign that St Elmo was protecting the ship from harm.

Erc(us)/Erghe/Erth. Various spellings. 31 October to 2 November.

Eric. 18 May. Scandinavian saint who is the patron of Sweden.

Erkenwald. 30 April.

Erkenwald, Translation of. 14 November.

Ernine. 28 February. Irish saint.

Erwan. 19 May. Saint of Brittany widely celebrated throughout Celtic Britain and considered the patron saint of lawyers.

Esther. Jewish fast.

Etheldreda. 23 June. Also known as St Audrey. She was an abbess and patron saint of Ely and Cambridge University. She is depicted with a staff (in bud) and a book in religious icons. Historically she is known to have been twice married, firstly to Tonbert who gave her the Isle of Ely as a dowry. He died three years after their marriage which appears to have been one only of convenience as she continued to live her life as a nun. A similar situation existed when she married King Ecgfrith of Northumberland who was totally unsatisfied with his wife's insistence on living a nun's life. She served at Coldingham and later founded a dual monastery for males and females at Ely, becoming its abbess for seven years before dying in 679.

Etheldreda, Translation of. 17 October. When her body was examined at her reburial, circa 695, she was said to look exactly as she did the day she was buried 16 years before.

Ethelwold. Date uncertain. Former Bishop of Winchester.

Eugenia. 16 March.

Eunurches. 7 September. He was also known as Evortius and was a Bishop of Orleans. His feast day was added to the English calendar in 1604, possibly to continue the feast day previously kept for Queen Elizabeth's Birthday.

Euphemia. 16 September.

Eusebius. 14 August.

Eustace. 2 November.

Eventius. 3 May.

Evortius. See under Eunurchus.

Ewen. 3 May. Celtic saint of Brittany whose feast was celebrated widely elsewhere.

Ewenny. Celtic saint. Also known as Aventi. Possibly the same as St Ewen.

Exaltation of the Holy Cross. 14 September. Represents the day when the true cross was erected on Mount Calvary in the 7th century by Heraclius. See also under Helena.

Expectation Sunday. The Sunday after Ascension Day.

Expulsion of Ghosts. 11 May. Pagan. See also under Helena.

Expulsion of Tarquin. See under Regifugium.

F

Fabian and Sebastian. 20 January.

Fabian, Bishop and Martyr. 20 January. It is said that when choosing the Bishop of Rome, a dove settled on his head whereupon which he was elected Pope and stayed as such for 16 years. He was martyred on 20 January 250.

Faelog. Festival date unknown. Celtic saint celebrated in Wales and elsewhere as St Maelog.

Fainche of Rossory. 1 January. Irish saint.

Faith. 6 October. She died as a child Christian martyr at Agen in Aquitania during the religious persecutions of Diocletian in 304. Though her prosecutor tried to advise her to deny her Christianity, she refused and was burned on a metal grate. In religious art form she is shown with a grate and a palm branch.

Fallen Fabii, Commemoration of. 13 February. Roman.

Faolan. 9 January. Irish.

Farting Monday. Coarse but commonly used name for the day after Carling Sunday (see under that entry).

Fasching Monday. See under Festival of Fools.

Fast Leaven (Fastelavn) Monday. See under Festival of Fools.

Fast of August. 23 August.

Fast of February. 1 February.

Fast of Friday. Every Friday in the year except when it fell on Christmas Day.

Fast of July. 24 July.

Fast of March. 24 March.

Fast of November. 29 November.

Fast of September. 20 September.

Fast of Thoth. 19 September. Pagan.

Fasting Monday. A corruption of Fasching Monday. See under Festival of Fools.

Fasts of December. 20 and 24 December.

Fasts of June. 23 and 28 June.

Fasts of October. 27 and 31 October.

Fata. 24 June. Roman festival.

Fat Tuesday. Tuesday before Lent.

Faunalia. 13 February and 1 December. Roman version of the Pagan festival of Faunus.

Faunicalia. Possibly the same festival as Faunalia. Fauns were a kind of rustic spiritual entity and the Italian half-goat mythical counterparts of the Greek satyrs such as Pan.

Faunus. 5 December (Pagan), 13 February (Roman).

Feast of ... See under Festival of ...

Feast of Feasts. Easter.

February Fast. 1 February.

February Fires. Pagan fire festivals which were transferred to the feasts of St Bridget, Candlemas and St Blaise. They survive as utility customs in country areas where burning of old heather, furze etc still takes place in February.

Feidhlimidh. 9 August. Irish saint with the full title of Feidhlimidh of County Cavan.

Felibrige. Ancient septennial festival originating in France involving travelling troubadours who entertained wherever they travelled.

Felicissmus and Agapitus. 6 August.

Felicitas. 17 January and 9 October. Roman festivals.

Felicity. 23 November.

Felicity and Perpetua. 7 March.

Felix. 14 January.

Felix and Audactus. 30 August.

Felix and Faunstinus. 29 July.

Feralia. Moveable January fair time that possibly coincided with Agnolia (Roman). In ancient Rome and its territories, Feralia was celebrated on 21 February and was dedicated to Jupiter.

Feriae Marti. Full month of March. This extended Roman festival incorporated within it a number of other festivals. It was dedicated to Mars.

Feronia. 15 November. One-day festival as part of the Roman Plebian Games.

Festival of Archangels. 29 September.

Festival of Camps. 2 November.

Festival of Flags. 5 May.

Festival of Fools (Roman). 1 May. Possibly the same as Fools' Holy Day. The Festival of Fools was a Roman festival when all the rules of society could be broken. Naked processions took place. In medieval times the feast was still celebrated but participants were by then wearing 'skin suits' made of white leather.

Festival of Fools (UK). Another name for Shrove Monday (see under that entry). It was also called Fasching or Fashing Monday and Fast Leaven (Fastelavn) Monday, in areas with foreign immigrants from Germany or Scandinavia. The festival dates back to at least Roman times when it was celebrated on either 1 or 17 February and was specifically meant for those who had not taken part in the Floralia festivities.

Festival of Joy. 25 March.

Festival of Light(s). 1 February, also 12 August. The Hindu version of the Festival of Light is called Divali, and the Jewish one Hannukkah.

Festival of Lots. Jewish festival also called Purim and celebrated on 14th Adar, four weeks before Passover. Celebrated with religious readings.

Festival of the Ass. 14 January.

Festival of the Dead. 1 November.

Festival of the Earth Mother. 1 February.

Festival of the Flowers. 1 May.

Festival of the Grain. 1 August

Festival of the Great Mother. 4 to 10 April.

Festival of the Vine. 21 September (Autumn Equinox).

Festival of Venus. 19 March

Festival of Weeks. Jewish version of Whitsuntide.

Festival of Zetesis. 28 October. Pagan.

Ffraid. 1 February. One of the few female Welsh saints.

Ffwst. Feast day uncertain. Survives in the Welsh place-name, Llanfoist.

Fianait. 4 January and 29 November. Irish.

Fides. 1 October. Roman festival.

Fillan. 25 June. St Fillan was related to St Kentigern(a) and St Comgan.

Fin(n)barr. 25 September. Irish saint also called Fionnbharr and possibly the same saint as Barr. See also under Barr(i).

Finian. Celtic saint who educated St Columba at Moville c.537.

Finnsech of Co. Tyrone. 13 October. Irish saint.

Finnsech of Co. Meath. 17 February. Irish saint.

Fintan. Celtic saint who was a relative of St Columba. Also called St Munnu.

Fionnbharr. See under Finnbarr.

Firebrand Sunday. First Sunday in Lent. Also called Brandon or Branding Sunday and Spark Sunday.

Fire Festivals. There were many of these but the 'Four Great Pagan Fire Festivals' were Samhain, Beltain, Lugnasad and Oimelc. See under these entries.

Firminus. 25 September.

Flags, Feast of. 5 May.

Floral Day. 1 or 8 May. Possibly originally a week-long festival as it is the modern-day version of the festival of Helith.

Florentian. See under Isidore.

Floria/Floralia. 27 April to 3 May. Roman festival honouring Flora the goddess of Spring and flowers. It dates back hundreds of years before Christianity and still survives in the Christianised festivals of Pentecost and May Day.

Flowers, Festival of. 1 May.

Fontinalia. 13 October. Roman festival dedicated to Fontus.

Fools' Holy Day. 1 May. See also Festival of Fools.

Fordicidia. 15 April. A Roman festival to celebrate the Earth goddess Tellus when pregnant cows were slaughtered as a sacrifice. The cows were eaten and the unborn young burnt and ploughed into the soil to ensure corn fertility.

Fornacalia/Fornicalia. 19 January to 17 February. Long Roman February festival period in honour of the god Fornax which had a number of other festivities intertwined with it. See also Fornax, below.

Fornax. 17 February. Specific day dedicated to Fornax in the Roman festival of Fornacalia which was itself a Fornax festival but with other festivities included within it. See under Fornacalia, above.

Fors Fortuna. 24 June. Roman festival.

Fortuna. 5 April, also 11 June. Roman festival.

Fortuna Redux. 12 October. Roman festival.

Fortuna Virilis. See under Veneralia.

Four Great Fire Festivals. See under Fire Festivals.

Francis (Borgia). 10 October. Patron saint of the Portuguese.

Francis (of Assisi). 4 October. Patron saint of animals, merchants and Italy. He was born 1182, the son of a travelling cloth merchant who insisted on calling him Francesco (Frenchman) rather than his given name of John. He travelled widely as a penniless monk, having given away all his possessions, and founded the Franciscan Order. He always encouraged all his followers to be jolly and friendly to all they met including birds and animals and the monks became known as God's Jesters (*Joculatores Domine*). He died on the evening of 3 October 1226. Legend says that birds flocked to the roof of the building in which he passed away. St Francis is depicted in a brown corded habit with the marks of the crucifixion on his hands, side and feet. See also under Stigmata.

Francis (of Paola). 2 April. A patron saint of sailors.

Francis (of Rome). 9 March.

Francis (of Sales). 29 January. Modern day saint who was born in 1567 and died 1662. He donated his body for anatomical research. He is the patron saint of writers and journalists.

Francis, Translation of. 25 May.

Francis Xavier. 2 December. Francis (1506-1552), the young son of Juan de Jasso, a Spanish nobleman, took his second name Xavier from his mother in the traditional Spanish style. He studied at Paris University and became a Master of Arts in 1530. He travelled throughout the world and sailed from Lisbon, Portugal for the East on 17 April 1541, the day his friend Ignatius Loyola began the Jesuit Order. His journeys took him to Africa, India and even Japan as a Jesuit missionary. On 25 April 1551 he sailed from Goa on a mission to China but died on board his ship, the *Santa Cruce*, off the island of San Chan, on 2 December 1552. He was only 120 miles from his goal, having succumbed to a fever.

Friday Fast. Every Friday in the year except when it fell on Christmas Day.

Frideswide (Abbess). 19 October. St Frideswide died 735 and is the patron saint of Oxford. She is generally depicted with a crown and an ox, but also as an abbess carrying a crook and a model of her convent in Oxford. Historically she was the daughter of a Mercian prince from Oxford. Algar, another prince, invaded Oxford in order to forcibly marry her but she escaped with other nuns in a boat. A fountain at Binsey is said to be the one from which she drank during her period of hiding. She spent the rest of her years teaching and healing the poor in a chapel that later became the present cathedral. Her tomb, which became a great place of pilgrimage, was robbed by Henry VIII and her bones were extracted, to

St Frideswide – Founded a convent at Oxford from which she is said to have fled in a boat, rowed by an angel.

be replaced by the body of Peter Martyr, the reformer. Queen Mary later reversed the procedure, re-interring Frideswide's bones. Queen Elizabeth is said to have placed both sets of bones in the Cathedral and her remains are now at rest in Christ Church, Oxford.

Fulgentius. See under Isidore.

Fulk/Fulco. 22 May. English saint of the 11th/12th century. He died at Alquin whilst on a pilgrimage.

Furrinalia. 25 July. Pagan festival first celebrated in Rome in honour of Furrina.

Furry Day (Floral Day). 1 or 8 May. Once generally celebrated but now the only vestige is the Furry Dance of Helston in Cornwall where couples dance through the streets. Doors are left open and shops and gardens are invaded by the dancers. One version of the song that accompanied the dance is as follows:

*Robin Hood and
   Little John will
   go to the Merry
   Greenwood-o*
*For to chase-o, to
   chase-o, to chase
   the buck and the
   doe-o*
*And we are up at
   dawn-o, to fetch
   the May blossom
   home-o*
*The summer is a
   come-o and the
   winter it is gone*
*With a heel and toe,
   jolly rumbelow*

Furry Day (Floral Day) – The Three Furies are shown above on a Greek bas-relief held at the Museum at Argos, Greece in 1900. The Phyrigian coin shown also depicts the three Furies, this time as vestal virgins, carrying candles.

It is highly likely that the festival has connection with the Roman reverence for the Furies. These were the Helenic deities, Alecto, Tisaphone and Megaera. The Greeks knew them as the Erinytes or Umenides who shared identities with the fates (known as Parcae). Votive offerings were made to the Three Furies by the Romans and dancing of the vestal virgins took place during the ceremonies.

G

Gabriel, Archangel. 24 March. Archangel Gabriel of the Annunciation is the patron saint of postmen and all communicators. His emblem is a lily.

Gall. Date uncertain. Gall accompanied St Columba to France and founded the monastery of St Gall in Switzerland where a manuscript telling of the life of St Gregory was found.

Gamaliel. 4 August.

Gamelia Festival. 1 January. Pagan.

Garbhan. 9 July. Irish saint.

Garmon. 3 July. Celtic saint.

Gasty/Gasteyn. Unknown feast day. Welsh.

Gaudette Sunday. The third Sunday in Advent.

Gedalia. Jewish fast day.

Genesius. 25 August. Patron saint of actors who has been recognised since Roman times.

Genevieve. 3 January. French saint (patron of Paris) who is also the patron saint of actors, lawyers and secretaries.

Geola. 21 December. Anglo-Saxon word for 'yoke'.

George. 23 April. St George is always depicted as a knight carrying a shield with a red cross (or a banner with a red cross), generally sitting upon a horse and always killing a dragon. As well as being the patron saint of England and Genoa, he is also the patron of rocky and dangerous coastlines, the mentally ill, places liable to flood, chivalrous knights, cavalrymen and soldiers. His feast day is observed over a wide part of the world, not only in English-speaking countries. He was martyred in Asia Minor in 303 and is said to have been canonised after Crusaders brought back stories of how he had assisted the English in battle. Historically it is believed he was born at Lydda, Palestine, into a wealthy family. He is often confused with George, the Cappadocian bishop who was lynched about 60 years after St George's death by torture and beheading. St George is buried at Lydda where a chapel was built over his tomb.

Gereon. 10 October.

German/Germaine/Germanus. 31 July. He was from a Christian family in Auxerre but was educated in Rome, becoming a Duke or Governor of the city. Here he upset other Christians by hanging up the heads of animals he had hunted for display. He is said to have become a changed man when he was persuaded to become a bishop and eventually travelled to Britain, traditionally landing at St Germains in Cornwall. German was said to have become involved in political as well as religious schisms, one such incident being the Alleluia Victory at Maesgarmon (Field of German) near Mold in Wales, where the Britons were victorious. He died a respected man on 31 July 448 at Ravenna, Italy, where he had gone to investigate the rebellion of the Amoricans.

Gertrude. 17 March. A Frenchwoman of noble birth, Gertrude was said to be great aunt to either Charles the Great or Charlemagne. She became a nun, with her mother, at Nivelles when her father died. She is frequently depicted in religious icons with a mouse nibbling at her staff, a reference to her thorough concentration whilst praying, excluding all outside distractions. She was at one time the patron saint of travellers because she was said to have had a particular affinity with the poor and wayfarers during her lifetime. She died in 664.

Gervais and Prothasius. 19 June.

Gesling Day. 1 May. See under Gosling Day.

Ghosts, Expulsion of. 11 May. Pagan.

Gidas. 29 January. Welsh saint.

Gil of Santiem. 14 May.

Gilbert of Caithness. 1 April. Bishop of Caithness, he lived at Dornoch, Scotland and died 1246.

Gilbert of Sempringham. 4 February. Founded the Gilbertine Order, the only truly British monastic movement.

Gilbert, Translation of. 13 October.

Giles/Gillies. 1 September. St Giles, abbot and hermit, is depicted as an old man in his monk's robes with a hind (female red deer) at his feet. He died in 712 and is the patron saint of beggars and cripples. Oddly, he is also considered a patron of blacksmiths and was known as St Egidius and Eligius/Eloi with a different festival day (see also under Eligius). Historically it is possible that he was a native of Athens but travelled widely across Europe. It was whilst living in a cave close to the Rhine that he saved a hind that was being attacked by hunters and suffered a mortal wound as a consequence. His feast day was celebrated widely in medieval Britain.

Gireg. 17 February. Saint of Brittany widely celebrated throughout Celtic Britain.

Gladez. 29 March. Female Celtic saint.

Glen. 11 September. Celtic saint of Brittany whose feast was celebrated throughout Britain.

Glewas. 3 May. Cornish Celtic saint. See also Gluvias, below.

Gluvias. 1 May, or first Sunday in May. Possibly a Christianisation of the Pagan feast of Gol/Goole/Gul/Gule celebrated in Cornwall and therefore probably the same as St Glewas whose feast day is 3 May.

Gobban of Killamery (Co. Meath). 11 October. Irish saint.

Gobnait. 11 February. Female Irish saint.

Godric (of Finchale). 18 December? Northumbrian saint who was a hermit, according to an account by Reginald, a monk of Durham (Surtees Soc. Vol 20. P365) and may well be the 12th century hermit who was slain whilst trying to defend wild animals from hunters at Eskdale Chapel near Sleights, Yorkshire. The incident is related to the planting of the '*Penny Hedge*' performed on Ascension Eve. See under Ascension.

Gog and Magog/Gogmagog. See under New Year's Day.

Gol. See under Gluvias.

Golden Number. See under Metonic Cycle.

Golden Rose. Celebrated the fourth Sunday in Lent. Originally a spring festival which became a ritualised religious rite. It was described as 'age-old' by Pope Leo IX (1049-54). It was once celebrated in Jerusalem but now only remains as a performed rite in the Vatican.

Goodfire Day (Beltane). 1 May.

Good Friday. Friday before Easter commemorating Christ's crucifixion. Also known as Holy Friday and Egyptian Day.

Good Shepherd Sunday. Second Sunday after Easter.

Gool(e). See under Gluvias.

Gordianus and Epimachus. 10 May.

Goron. 7 April. Cornish Celtic saint.

Gosling Day. 1 May. Still celebrated in some areas as 'May Gosling Day' in much the same way as April Fools' Day is celebrated elsewhere. Also known as Gesling Day in the north of England.

Gower. 15 November. Celtic saint also called Cywair.

Govren. 16 November. Celtic saint of Brittany celebrated throughout Britain.

Grain Festival. 1 August.

Great(er) Week. See under Holy Week.

Great Feast of the Dead. See under Samhain.

Great Friday. Good Friday.

Great Litany. See under Litania Major.

Great Mother. 4 April to 10 April. Pagan.

Great Sabbath. See under Holy Saturday.

Great St Hugh of Avalon. See under Hugh of Avalon and Hugh of Lincoln.

Great St Hugh of Lincoln. See under Hugh of Avalon and Hugh of Lincoln.

Green Thursday. See under Maundy Thursday.

Gregory the Great. 12 March. Pope Gregory also has the title 'Father of the Latin Church' and is the patron saint of musicians and scholars. He lived c.540-604 and is usually depicted holding his papal cross and with a dove near his ear. In 601 he sent missionaries throughout the world to Christianise pagan festivals. He is often known as Gregory Magnus. He is perhaps best commonly known for his remark about young British slaves that he saw for sale in a market place in Rome: '*These are not Angles, they are angels*'. His feast day marks the day of his burial, a day after his death.

Gregory the Great, Ordination of. 3 September.

Grimbald. 8 July.

Gudwell. Possibly St Gluvias, as a stained glass window to Gudwell was placed in a church window in St Gulval, Cornwall, though this would mean a change in gender. Also probably the same as St Wolvela. See under Gluvias.

Gul(e). See under Gluvias.

Gule of August. 1 August. Feast day when gluttony was encouraged. See also under Lammas.

Gulval. 12 November.

Gunpowder Plot. See Papist Conspiracy.

Guthlac. 11 April. A 12th century saint whose image is preserved on the Guthlac Roll in the Harley Roll (Y6.f13) in the British Museum.

Guy Fawkes Night. See Papist Conspiracy.

Gwen Teirbron. 18 October. Female Celtic saint.

Gwen(frewi). 3 November. Female Cornish Celtic saint.

Gwennec. 6 March. Saint of Brittany who was patron of Plouhinec. Widely celebrated throughout the Celtic world.

Gwenole. 3 March. Saint of Brittany widely celebrated throughout Celtic Britain.

Gwenrael. 23 December. Celtic.

Gwytherin. Feast day unknown. Welsh.

Gwynno. Feast day unknown. Welsh.

H

Haeddi. See under Hedda.

Hallow Fire. Scottish Hallowe'en practice of lighting fires or walking in procession with burning torches. It was recorded as surviving in Scotland in the mid 19th century.

Hallowe'en. 31 October.

Handsel Day. First Monday in January. Scottish.

Hannukkah. Also called Chanukah or Chanucah. December Jewish festival of light which commemorates the defeat of the Greeks by Judas Maccabaeus. In this festivity the normal seven-branched candlestick is replaced by one with eight candles. Food is served and gifts are exchanged.

Hans. 23 June.

Haran. Feast day unknown. Welsh.

Harvest Festival. 1 August (often the Sunday nearest).

Hedda. 7 July. Also known as St Haeddi, he was educated at Whitby Abbey before becoming Bishop of the West Saxons and is credited with making Winchester the former capital city of England. He died in 705 and was buried in Winchester Cathedral.

Heirarchs, Holiday of the Three. See under Three Heirarchs.

Heironymus. 30 September. Also known as St Jerome.

Harvest Festival – Even the smallest hamlets would celebrate the bringing home of the harvest, as shown in this 18th-century print.

Helen. 2 May. Also known as Witchwood Day. See under that entry.

Helena. 18 August and 21 May. Helena (248-327) was mother of the Emperor Constantine. At the age of 80, she went on a pilgrimage in search of the true holy cross on which Christ had died. This she is alleged to have found on 3 May 326. Both 3 May and 14 September are celebrated as the day the cross was found. Though early historians tell of the wood from the true cross being found, Helena is not mentioned as its discoverer until the year 400. See also under Holy Cross and Rood Day.

Helier. 16 July. Saint of the Channel Islands and patron saint of Jersey. He was of Belgian birth but as a monk came to Jersey and lived as a hermit in a cave above the town that now bears his name.

Helios. 25 December.

Helith. Ancient May festival that developed in Cornwall into the Furry or Floral Dance festival. Helith is connected with the god Hercules whose figure has associations with some ancient hill figures. See also under Hercules.

Henry V Day. 25 October.

Heodez. 28 November. Female Celtic saint.

Hercules. 3 May. A constituent part of the Roman festival of Bona Dea. See also under Helith. A single day festival by this name was also celebrated in Roman times on 12 August.

Hercules the Guardian. 4 June. Roman festival.

Hermenilda. 13 February.

Hermes. 28 August. Hermes Trismegistrus was considered the god of knowledge and wisdom. His sister and companion was Seshat, also known as the goddess Saf, who was anciently patron deity of archives and who was said to be patron of the former Great Library of Alexandria.

Herve. 17 June. Great Bardic Celtic saint of Brittany. Celebrated also in UK.

Hilary, Feast Day of. 13 January. Born of Pagan parents, he was made Bishop Hilary of Poitiers, was famed as a teacher and is said to have been sought out by St Martin for enlightenment. A profuse writer, he was banished to Phyrigia in 356 by the Emperor Constantius. He was allowed to return four years later and died in 368.

Hocktide – Tuttimen at Hungerford demanding their traditional Hocktide kiss from the women of the area in the 1930s. The illustration shows that the Tuttimen were not to be put off by ladies who had climbed to high vantage points in a bid to avoid their advances.

Hilary, Festival of. The period between the old festival of Michaelmas Day and that of St Thomas the Apostle. Traditionally the date when law sittings commenced.

Hilda, Death of. 17 November. Hilda died 17 November 680 aged 66 years. Her death is recorded both in Bede's *History* and in the *Anglo Saxon Chronicle*. A passage concerning a bell being tolled for her passing is the first written mention of a bell in recorded history.

Hilda, Festival of. 25 August. Hilda, or Hild, was of royal birth and after her father had been murdered she lived with her great-uncle, King Edwin of Northumbria, who she was baptised alongside at York at the age of 13. This was on the eve of Easter in 627. She became Abbess of Hartlepool and then of Whitby. She championed the Celtic cause against that of the Roman Church at the Synod of Whitby and accepted its findings even though they were opposed to her own views.

Hillaria. 25 March was the main day but the Roman festival extended from 22 March to 1 April. See also under Blood Days and May Day.

Hilledd. Feast day unknown. Welsh.

Hippolytus. 13 August. Elected anti-pope when he criticised Pope Zephyrinus in the 3rd century. Patron saint of horses due to a confusion with the legend of his Greek namesake, son of Diana. Diana's feast day is also commemorated on 13 August.

Hippolytus (Roman). 20 June. Roman horse festival.

Hock Day. Second Tuesday after Easter.

Hocktide. Early festival of mirth around Hock Day when various local customs were performed, as at Hungerford where 'Tuttimen' otherwise known as 'Tithe Men' traditionally enacted the 'Hock Tide Court'. From the Middle Ages a band of men would demand a coin from every male over twelve years old and a kiss from every female.

Hogmanay. 31 December. See under New Year's Day.

Hogmagog. See under New Year's Day.

Hogunnaa. 31 December.

Holi. Hindu Spring festival celebrated in late February or early March with bonfires and the throwing of coloured water or confetti. Nuts and chickpeas are traditionally roasted on the bonfires.

Holly King. Ancient festival to celebrate Midwinter's Day. A similar festival was held to celebrate midsummer and was called the festival of the Oak King.

Holy Cross Day. 14 September. See also under Helena, Rood Day and Triumph of the Cross.

Holy Cross, Exaltation of. 14 September. See also under Helena.

Holy Eucharist. See under Passover.

Holy Fools' Day. 1 April. Originally a church festival but now translated to April Fools' Day or All Fools' Day when jokes are played upon friends until 12 noon when, if the time is not noticed, the one playing the prank is designated a fool.

Holy Friday. Another name for Good Friday.

Holy Innocents. 28 December. See under Childermas.

Holy Name of Mary. 12 September. See also under Virgin Mary.

Holy Rood Day. The same as Holy Cross Day (see under that entry).

Holy Saturday. Saturday before Easter. It was also known as Easter Even and the Great Sabbath.

Holy Thursday. Day before Good Friday when in many areas the ceremony of the Beating of the Bounds took place in order to remind everyone where a town's or land-owner's boundaries were situated. See also under Ascension.

Holy Week. The week preceding Easter Sunday. It was also called Great(er) Week, Passion Week, Week of Forgiveness and Paschal Week. See also Tenebrae.

Homobonus. 13 November. Homobonus, the 'good man', was a 12th century lay preacher who seems to have achieved no great degree of holiness other than that he was a man of great generosity. He was made a saint only two years after he collapsed in church whilst preaching and fell face down on the altar cross, dead. He was a businessman in life and became the patron saint of all in business.

Honoratus (of Amiens). 16 May. A 6th century Bishop of Amiens who was born in nearby Port-le-Grand and died in 600. Patron saint of bakers and flour merchants. In art he is often shown with tools of these trades.

Honorius. 30 September.

Horn(ing) Day. 8 September.

Horn Dance Day. 9 September.

Horonina. 27 February.

Horse Ribbon Day. 1 May. Northern version of May Day, when horses and carts were dressed up in striped ribbons.

Horus. 25 December.

Horus (slaying of Set). 23 April.

Hoshana Rabba. Jewish celebration.

Hugh of Avalon. 12 March and 17 November. Often confused with Hugh of Lincoln. Hugh of Avalon's emblem is a swan. He was the son of a nobleman who was lord of the castle of Avalon. When Hugh's mother died, his father retired to the monastery of Villarbenoit, taking Hugh with him. He became a monk, eventually joining the community at Grande Chartreuse where he stayed for about 15 years. He lived a life of true austerity, wearing only hair shirts, taking part in vigils and fasts and engaging in self-flagellation. When he did eat, he survived on bread and water which is said to have made him exceedingly fat. He later became Bishop of Lincoln and was said to have spoken 'man to man' with Henry II, Richard I and King John, each of whom he mentally dominated. Despite his domineering character, he was devout and kindly, loving animals as well as men. His relationship with animals was demonstrated by a Lincoln swan which would follow him like a dog whenever he visited the city. The swan that he loved in life appears on many religious paintings representing him. On 18 September 1200 he was taken ill whilst in London and was taken to the Temple where he had a house. He died there two months later (on Thursday 16 November). Having asked to be buried in

St Hugh of Avalon, 1135–1200 – Bishop of Lincoln.

Lincoln, a great procession followed his cortege through London. King John acted as pall bearer for part of the journey and many bishops, abbots, knights and Jews attended his funeral. His grave within Lincoln Cathedral has never been disturbed.

Hugh of Liege. 3 November. Patron saint of hunters and victims of rabies. Said to have died c.1200.

Hugh of Lincoln. 17 November. Often confused with Hugh of Avalon.

Hugh, Translation of. 6 October.

Huntigowok Day. 1 April. Scottish version of All Fools' or April Fools' Day.

Hwita Sunnandaeg. Whit Sunday (Old English for White Sunday).

Hypapante. See under Candlemas.

Hypolit. 13 August.

I

Iago. 25 July. Celtic version of festival of St James.

Ibor. 23 April. Irish saint known as St Ibor of Beggerin Island.

Ide. 15 January. Female Irish saint.

Ides. The 15th day of March, May, July and October and the 13th of other months (Roman calendar).

Ifinus. Feast day unknown. Irish saint. His church (ruined) near Glendalough was later referred to as Our Lady's Church.

Ignatius. 1 February, also 31 July. Bishop of Antioch who was also called Theophorus, meaning 'one who carries God in his heart'. He was martyred as a Christian, having been thrown to the wild animals in the Coliseum at Rome in 107.

Ignatius Loyola. 31 July (evening festival). Born between 1491 and 1495, he was the founder of the Society of Jesus and is the patron saint of all those who retire to a religious retreat. In 1534, he founded the 'Brotherhood of Jesus', also known as the 'Society of Jesus', and commonly called the Jesuits, with the aim of defending Catholicism against the Reformation.

Ildephonsus. 23 January.

Illteyrn. Feast day unknown. Welsh.

Imbolc or Imbolg. 1-2 February. Pagan version of Candlemas.

Immaculate Conception. 8 December. To celebrate the Virgin Mary's deliverance from original sin after the birth of Christ.

Immaculate Heart of Mary. 22 August.

Innocents, Holy. 28 December.

Invention of the Holy Cross. 3 May. See under Rood Day.

Ireneus. 5 July.

Isadore. 2 January.

Isidore/Isidro. 4 April. A bishop of Seville, he was originally a farmer and became patron saint of all farmers. His brothers Leander, Florentian and Fulgentius were also saints.

Isis. 14 April. Pagan.

Ithon. 14 April. Ancient goddess figure, possibly related to worship of Isis.

J

Jack in the Green Parade. Parade that once took place in London on May Day with chimney sweeps dressed in elaborate 'costumes' made of woven branches, leaves and natural greenery.

James the Apostle (the Greater). 25 July. Brother, some claim half-brother, of Christ and brother of St John, the son of Zebedee and Salome. He is often confused with James the Lesser who some scholars believe to be the same person. He is said to have been the first Bishop of Jerusalem and was trusted by both Jews and Christians. He was the author of the Epistle of St James and is said to have died by stoning, finally being dispatched with a fuller's club, so causing the siege of Jerusalem. He was finally beheaded and his body was put on a ship at Jaffa (AD 43) and shipped to Spain, to be buried at Compostella in the north. The tomb became a place of pilgrimage and the town still draws pilgrims to this day. He is the patron saint of Spain and is said to appear on a white horse whenever the country is in danger. In religious art he is depicted by, or with, a scallop shell and often also with a sword and pilgrim's staff. See also Iago.

James the Less(er). 1 May. He was also known as James the Little to distinguish him from James the Apostle, who was the brother of Jesus. Both Jameses' mothers were called Mary, though James the Lesser's mother was the wife of Cleophas, also known as Alphaeus. James the Lesser may well be the brother of St Matthew. Mary his mother is said to have stood at the foot of the cross when Christ was crucified. There is much confusion over this saint's life, not least because he mysteriously shares a feast day with St Philip the Apostle.

Janbryght. 12 August.

Janmashtami. Celebrated at midnight between August and September (eighth day of Shravan) to commemorate the birth of Lord Krishna, the eighth incarnation of God. At midnight a conch shell is blown and a cradle is revealed which is traditionally showered by the celebrants with rose petals, beads, sweets and dried fruits celebrating the end of the fast.

Januarius. 19 September.

Janus. 21 May and 11 December, also 22 December. Pagan. Though the main festival celebrating Janus was Agonalia (see under that entry), he was also venerated in May (a spring festival) and December. Feast days were also held on the Summer and Winter Solstices on or around 21 June and 21 December in the modern calendar (see under those entries). This variation in his commemoration is due to a number of factors including changes of calendar, moveable feasts and the fact that he was the god of the beginning and end (of all things). Janus was described as 'the one who knows' and with his two faces could see all aspects of everything. He was the patron of all new undertakings and the god of transition. The Romans considered him the guardian of all things and placed his statue at the gates of temples and buildings. His name was chosen for the first month of the calendar (January) and his year of reign was said to begin on 6 January and end on 5 January, the end of the Old Style year. In Roman times initiation ceremonies always used his name and young people entering adult life were given tokens bearing his image. Tradition says that he came from Thessaly and that he shared the kingdom of Latinium with Camise his wife. He had a number of children including Tiber. Janus and his wife lived on the hill of Janiculum. He is credited with the invention of money and agriculture. Roman temples to Janus were only open during times of war, at other times they remained closed. In Christianity the two-faced Janus became John (or rather two Johns: St John the Evangelist and St John the Baptist). It is interesting to note that Janus and John the Baptist have commemorative festivals around the Summer Solstice, just as Janus and John the Evangelist share festivals around the Winter Solstice. See also Agonalia.

Jarlath. 6 June. Irish saint.

Jerome (Cardinal). 30 September. Listed as a Father of the Latin Church. His emblem is a lion and he is depicted wearing a cardinal's cap and carrying a book. He is the patron saint of students and libraries and was also known as St Hieronymus. Historically he is thought to have been born at Stridon on the border of Pannonia and Dammatia in the year 331. Coming from a wealthy family, he trained as a lawyer, went to Rome and lived a wild lifestyle. During a period of illness in Antioch in 374 he is said to have had a religious vision. He began then to study Hebrew and was eventually made a priest. Whilst in Rome, he became unpopular and left to visit Palestine with a female companion named Paula. They visited Egypt and finally settled at Bethlehem where Jerome built a monastery and Paula a convent nearby. Whilst at the monastery he translated the Bible and gave us the modern Vulgate. Jerome is perhaps unique in that during his lifetime he was not popular, being argumentative and subject to relatively loose living. He died on 30 September 419 and was buried in Bethlehem. Later his remains were translated to Rome.

Jesus, Name of. 7 August.

Joachim. It is said that an angel appeared to St Anne and St Joachim to announce the miraculous birth of the Virgin Mary, after which they dedicated Mary to the service of the Temple as a Vestal Virgin until the time of her marriage to Joseph.

Sts Anne and Joachim – Parents of the Virgin Mary.

Joan (of Arc). 30 May. Patron saint of France but connected with Britain through the alliance between the Burgundians and England. She actually fought the English on the French side, was caught and pleaded guilty in exchange for a pardon from the church. Her pardon was blocked by the English and she then withdrew her confession. Her actions ensured she was burned at the stake, supposedly for witchcraft, but was later declared free of guilt by the Church in 1455 and was canonised in 1920. Her ashes were said to have been thrown into the Seine by the English to prevent any relics being given to churches in her memory. She lived 1412 to 1431.

John and Paul. 26 June.

John Before the Latin Gate. 6 May. Commemorates the legend that St John the Divine was thrown into a bath of boiling oil in Rome and escaped unhurt. See also under John the Evangelist.

John Chrysostom. 27 January. Former Bishop of Constantinople who died 407. The title 'Chrysostom' means 'Golden Mouth' and referred to his eloquence. He trained as a lawyer but was baptised at 23 years old and later entered a religious community at Antioch where he wrote voluminously. He is alleged to have been kidnapped in order to get him to accept the position of Bishop of Constantinople which he had refused for some time. He was, however, exiled in 404 and died aged 60. His body was later translated to Constantinople.

John of Beverley (Bishop). 7 May. He was first admitted to the monastery of Whitby under Abbess Hild (Hilda) and then was consecrated to the See of Hagulstad (Hexham), moving later to York. He retired to Beverley where he lived a solitary life.

John of Beverley, Translation of. 25 October.

John (the Almoner). See under John the Baptist, Beheading of.

John the Baptist, Beheading of. 29 August. St John was beheaded this day by King Herod in AD 30. St John was and is the patron saint of the Order of the Knights of St John. He replaced St John the Almoner during the early days of the Crusades.

John the Baptist, Nativity of. 24 June. The patron saint of farriers (and of tailors and missionaries). He is usually depicted wearing animal skins and carrying both a cross and a lamb. See also under Janus.

John the Evangelist (The Divine). 27 December and 6 May. Patron of publishers, artists, printers, booksellers and all who deal in printed matter in any way. He is always depicted with (or as) an eagle and a book and often with (or as) a serpent with a chalice. John was said to be Christ's favourite disciple and that as such he was given a secret spoken message. Some say that 'oral secrets' have been transmitted down to modern times by an invisible movement within Christianity whose members share a 'deeper understanding'. Whether or not this is true, St John the Evangelist was said to be the favourite writer of Gnostics and he is still the patron saint of a number of 'secret societies'. Some have claimed that churches connected to the veneration of St John the Evangelist were always built with round ends and that every church dedicated to St Peter should have a church dedicated to St John nearby. A close look at the names of rounded churches and those named after St Peter should reveal just how widely these esoteric traditions have spread. Historically, John the Divine was the brother of James. Both were sons of Zebedee. John the Divine is

St Peter and St John – Depicted together at the gates of the temple in Jerusalem.

said to have opposed the heretic, Cerinthus, at Ephesus and to have refused to enter the public baths when he was present. He is said to have lived to an extremely old age and to have amused himself with a pet partridge when he was unable to read because of bad eyesight. See under John before the Latin Gate, also under Janus.

John's Eve. 23 June.

Jose. 13 December.

Jose, Translation of. 9 January.

Joseph (Father of Christ). 19 March. Depicted carrying or leading the Christ child. He is the patron saint of family life, carpenters and engineers. Tradition says that he was of royal descent and was a widower when he married Mary. A cult to Joseph had many followers in the Middle Ages and as late as 1871, Pope Pius IX proclaimed him patron of the whole Church.

Joseph of Arimathea. 17 March. The exact relationship of Joseph of Arimathea to Christ is a subject for controversy, some saying he is the brother of Christ, some Christ's uncle. He is generally accepted as a Sanhedrin and a disciple of Christ. Many believe he was a rich tin merchant who travelled regularly to Cornwall. He is said to have travelled to the isle of Avalon (now Glastonbury Hill?) where he planted his staff which became a tree and still blooms annually at Christmas (the Glastonbury thorn). It was Joseph who was said to have brought the infant Jesus, or controversially, Jesus the son of Jesus and Mary Magdalene, to England. This is said to be referred to in the well loved British hymn, *Jerusalem*. See also under Mary Magdalene.

Joseph of Cupertino. 18 September. A modern day saint born at Cupertino, Italy in 1603 (died 1663). He became a priest in 1628 and gained a reputation for miracles, healing the sick and levitating. Consequently he was accepted as the patron saint of all who fly.

Joy, Festival of. 25 March.

Jude (Apostle). 28 October. Depicted with an axe or a club, St Jude is the patron saint of lost causes and those in desperate situations. It was common in the past to evoke his name for deliverance from tragic circumstances such as pending ship-wrecks. Historically he has been confused with Judas Iscariot as he was also known as Judas, but Jude is certainly a different person. His real name was probably Judas Lebbaeus Thaddaes and he was believed by many to be a brother of Jesus, as the opening passage of the Bible's General Epistle of Jude begins: '*Jude the servant of Jesus Christ and brother of James...*'. See also under Simon and Jude.

Judica (Sunday). See under Passion Sunday.

Judikael. 16 December. Celtic.

Jul. 21 December. Norwegian word for 'wheel' and pronounced 'Yul'.

Julian. 27 January.

Juliana. 23 February.

Juliana (Martyr). 16 February.

Juliot. Date uncertain. Cornish saint who is believed to have founded the early monastic settlement at Tintagel.

July Fast. 24 July.

June Fasts. 23 and 28 June.

Juno. 1 to 7 January. Roman festival. A shorter festival with the same name was also held on 1 and 2 June. See under Matronalia and Nonae Caprotinae. Also 13 November when it was celebrated as a one-day festival as part of the Roman Plebian Games.

Juno Sopista. 1 and 2 February. Part of the Roman festival of Fornacalia.

Jupiter. 15 March. One-day festival dedicated to Jupiter during the month-long Roman festival of Feriae Marti. See also Poplifugia. Also 13 November, when it was celebrated as a one-day festival as part of the Roman Plebian Games.

Just. 10 November.

Justina, Martyrdom of. 26 September.

Justitia. 8 January. Roman festival.

Juturna. 23 August. Roman festival.

Juturnalia. 11 January. Roman festival dedicated to Juturna.

Juvenalia. Special games for Roman children, instituted by Emperor Nero.

K

Kado. See under Cadoc.

Kali (Ma). See under Cailleach.

Kanna. 10 March. Female Celtic saint.

Kaourantin. 12 December. Female Celtic saint.

Karamu. See under Kwanzaa.

Katagogian. 24 January. Pagan. See under Timothy.

Katherine. 25 November. Though celebrated on the same day as St Catherine, the name when spelt with the letter K carries a mystical reference to earlier pagan rites at Elysium when dancing and cymbal clashing accompanied the 'procession of the ark' from Cariathiarim (Kirjath Jearim). See also under Catherine.

Kavan. 10 March. Saint of Brittany widely celebrated throughout Celtic Britain.

Kea. Feast day unknown. Cornish.

Kenelm. 17 July.

Kenneth. See under Cainnech.

Kentigern(a). 14 January. Scottish saint who was a former bishop and is now patron saint of Glasgow. Also known as Mungo, a nickname meaning 'dearest', given to him by St Servan. It was she who baptised him. He died in 601 (or 612?) at an advanced age. He was known by the Celts as Conthigerni and by the Welsh as Cyndeyrn (the Hound-Lord). See also Fillan.

Kessog. Feast day unknown. Saint of the Scottish Highlands.

Kevern. 18 November. Cornish Celtic saint.

Kevin. 3 June. St Kevin lived as a hermit in a valley near Glendalough, Ireland. Also called Coemgen, he was sent, aged seven, to a monastery where he served with monks who later became St Lochanus, St Eighan and St Enna, and had previously been to school with St Petroc. He died in 618 and is said to have lived to 120 years.

Kieran. Irish Celtic saint who was founder of Clonmacnoise. The remains of the church dedicated to him were rediscovered in 1875 near Glendalough.

Killian. 3 July. Irish saint and former abbot of Iona. See also under Cronan.

King Charles I (the Martyr). 30 January. King and Martyr 1600-1649, he is said to have stated: '*Let my condition be never so low, I resolve by the Grace of God, never to yield up this church to the government of Papists, Presbyterians, or Independents.*' He was sentenced to death during the English Civil War on Saturday 27 January 1649 and was later buried at St George's Chapel, Windsor. His feast day was first celebrated in 1662. It was removed from the official list of church ceremonies in 1859.

King Charles II. 29 May.

King Edward, Trial of. 20 June

Kirn Festival. Harvest festival (Scotland). The word 'kirn' means kirk, or church, and is not related to the word corn. In some areas 'kirn babies' or 'corn dollies' were made from the last sheaf of corn. These were taken to the kirk and hung up until the following harvest festival.

Klervi. 3 October. Female Celtic saint.

Knut's Day. 19 January. See under Canute.

Konan. 28 September. Saint of Brittany widely celebrated throughout Celtic Britain.

Koulma. 25 February. Female Celtic saint.

Krishna. See under Janmashtami.

Kristen. 12 November. Female Celtic saint.

Kwanzaa. 26 December to 1 January. Celebrated by the African community in Britain as a Christmas festival, but in their homeland as a harvest festival. It involves the lighting of seven candles representing the principles of Nguzo Saba dealing with various aspects of co-operation, faith and creativity. The final night of festivities is called Karamu.

L

Laa'l Breeshey. Eve of 1 February. Ireland and Isle of Man.

Lady Day. 25 March.

Laetare Sunday. Fourth Sunday of Lent, also called Mid-Lent Sunday and Mothering Sunday. Laetare means 'rejoice' hence its other name, 'Rejoicing Sunday'. It was also known colloquially as 'Refreshment Sunday'.

Lakshmi. Her day is celebrated at Divali, the five-day festival of lights. Lakshmi is the goddess of wealth who demands purity and cleanliness from all Hindus.

Lambert. Bishop and Martyr. 17 September. Born of a noble Maestricht family around 636, he was made bishop of that town in 670. He was mysteriously murdered along with everyone in his household, c.709.

Lammas. 1 August. Said by some to celebrate the memory of St Peter's deliverance from imprisonment. A Christianised version of Lugnasad (see under that entry). Also called Loaf Mass, Gule of August and St Peter ad Vincula.

Lanfranc. 28 May.

Lantern Festival. See under Teng Chieh.

Larentia/Larentalia. 23 December. Roman festival dedicated to Acca and Larenta (equivalent to Lars/Laris, the Teutonic god of the home).

Lares, Compitalia of. 12 January. Roman festival.

Lares Praestitites. 1 May. Roman.

Lassa(air) of Meath. 8 February. Irish saint.

Last Sunday (after Pentecost). 24th Sunday after Pentecost.

Latare Sunday. See under Laetare Sunday and Lent.

Laudes Sunday. See under Low Sunday.

Laurence. See under Lawrence.

Laurence (O'Toole). 14 November. Irish saint who was ordained in 1157 as 'Abbot of the Glen' after he refused to be bishop because of his age. In 1180, after returning from Rome, he visited England to plead on behalf of the Irish chiefs but died at Eu Abbey in the same year on 14 November.

Laurentalia. 23 December. Pagan.

Lawrence (Martyr). 10 August. He is depicted in a deacon's gown and carrying a gridiron and/or a book. The gridiron represents that on which he was burnt to death in Rome in 258. He is patron saint of schoolboys, cooks, cutlers and those involved in manufacturing armour. His name was traditionally invoked by those seeking protection against damage by fire or by those suffering from rheumatism. He is said to protect vineyards from fire and lightning. The latter protection no doubt stems from his festival date coinciding with the Perseid meteor showers. In Italy, where he is known as San Lorenzo, the evening of the showers is called La Notre di San Lorenzo (the Night of St Lawrence).

St Lawrence – The martyred St Lawrence is usually depicted with the gridiron on which he was flayed to death.

Lea. 15 November. Cornish Celtic saint.

Leander. See under Isidore.

Leger. 2 October.

Lemura (Expulsion of Ghosts). 9-13 May. The festival dates back at least to Roman times and had its main day on 11 May (11 being a magical number). See Lemuria, below.

Lemuria. 7-15 May. Roman festival of the dead. (See also under Lemura above)

Lent. Forty day fast lasting from Ash Wednesday to Easter. It was tradition for confirmation ceremonies to take place during Lent and Lenten suppers were often prepared. 'Lent' is Old English for Spring. It was also known as Carneval, said to mean 'evaluation of the meat ration' and may well have been a time when meat was forbidden to be eaten whilst an evaluation of livestock was made.

Lent – Newly confirmed boys attending a Lenten Supper in 1900.

Leo. 28 June.

Leo the Great. 11 April. Leo served as Pope from 449 until his death. He met Attila the Hun at the gates of

Rome and succeeded in persuading him to spare the city. He died in 461 and is buried in the Church of St Peter, Rome.

Leonard. 6 November. He was the godson of Clovis, leader of the Franks, who was at first a cloistered monk, then a solitary hermit only to finally found a monastery of his own. He is said to have devoted his life to ransoming prisoners. This is reflected in religious art where he is often depicted wearing fetters and chains. He is the patron saint of prisoners and in former times it was common for ex-prisoners to hang up their chains in churches dedicated to St Leonard. He died circa 560.

Leri. 30 September. Celtic saint of Brittany whose feast was celebrated widely elsewhere.

Letardus. 7 May.

Levenez. 3 January. Female Celtic saint.

Liberalia. See under Bacchanalia.

Liberation Day. 9 May. Channel Islands.

Light (of Arthur). 21 December.

Lights Festival. 1 February, also 12 August.

Linus. 26 November.

Litania Minor. The 'Small Litany' or Rogation that occurred three days before Ascension. It replaced the Roman festival Ambarvalia which involved the sacrifice of a bull, a sheep and a pig which had been chased around the perimeter of a field by a procession of locals who finally encircled the animals. See under Rogation Sunday.

Litania Major. The 'Great Litany' which fell on St Mark's Day. It replaced the Roman Robigalia when red-haired puppies were sacrificed. See under Robigalia.

Litha. 21 June (Summer Solstice).

Little Aed. See under Dear Aed and Aed.

Little Christmas. 23 December. The day when domestic Christmas festivities began, particularly in areas of England with Viking connections. The day is still known as such in Denmark.

Livinus. 12 November.

Llolan. Date of festival not known. Celtic, probably Welsh saint. Believed to have undertaken missionary work to Scotland where his artifacts were traditionally held by the Earls of Perth.

Loaf Mass. Same as Lammas.

Lochanus. See under Kevin.

Loi (Bishop). See under Elgius.

Lolan. See under Llolan.

Lomman. 11 October. Irish saint, fully known as St Lomman of Trim (County Meath).

Lonan Finn. 22 January. Irish.

Long Friday. Anglo-Saxon name for Good Friday due to the long fast imposed upon that day.

Lorcan O Tuathail. 14 November. Irish saint.

Lord Mayor's Day. 9 November. Parade and celebrations during the annual installation of the City of London's Lord Mayor. It was once traditional for Lord Mayor's Day to be held on the feast of St Simon and St Jude (see under that entry.) In 1346, this was changed to 16 October and in 1546 this was again changed to Michaelmas Day. The swearing-in then continued to be held on 29 October until the calendar change of 1752 when 8 and 9 November were considered the correct days for the election and presentation, respectively.

Lothwick. Saint day unknown. Mentioned by Charlton in his *History of Whitby* (18th century) as being venerated at Whitby Abbey and being patron saint of horses there.

Louis. 25 August. He was the eldest son of Louis VIII of France and became king himself in 1226. He was said to have led a humble and compassionate life, yet was strong of mind. He joined the Crusade of 1267 but fell sick in Tunis and died 25 August 1270.

Low Sunday. Sunday after Easter Sunday, probably a corruption of Laudes Sunday. It was also known as Close Sunday, Dominica in Albis Deponendis and New Sunday.

Love Feast. See under Wakes.

Lucaria. 19-23 July. Roman festival to commemorate those who died when Rome was sacked by the Gauls and to celebrate the later defeat of the Gallic army.

Lucia. 13 October.

Luciadagann. 13 December. Viking festival which began Yuletide celebrations. Coincides with the feast of St Lucy.

Lucian. 8 January. Born at Samosata c.240 and spent most of his life in Antioch. A mystic, he was accused of heresy and was tortured by Maximian at Nicodemia. His last words in 312 were said to be 'I am a Christian, I am a Christian, I am a Christian'.

Lucian and Geminian. 16 September.

Lucy (Virgin and Martyr). 13 December. No doubt adapted from a pagan festival of light as her name means Lux (light). A legend tells that her eyes were plucked out yet miraculously her sight was restored. In real life she is associated with a martyr who, in 303, had her eyes burned out for refusing to renounce Christianity. A number of other 'eye' stories are associated with her and she is now the patron saint of those with eye problems. See also Christingle.

Ludi Apollinares. 5 July. Roman celebration in honour of Apollo, typified by the playing of games.

Ludi Consualia. 21 August. Roman chariot racing festival in honour of Consus, the god of politics, counsel and secret planning.

Ludi Magni. Began 4 September. The Great Roman Games of Ludi Magni were held in celebration of the gods Jupiter, Minerva and Juno.

Ludi Martiales. 12 May. Roman games festival honouring the god Mars.

Ludi Mercery. 15 May. Roman games festival in honour of the god Mercury.

Ludi Piscatori. 17 June. Roman swimming and fishing festival dedicated to Tiberinus and originally taking place in the river Tiber.

Ludi Romani. 5-19 September. Roman festival involving games and contests of all kinds.

Luercus. See under Lupercalia.

Lughnassa(dh). 1 August. Pagan pivotal point of the unstable spiritual world. It was one of the Four Great Fire Festivals (see under that entry). In Ireland it was known as *Lugh-Nasadh*, *Lunes Day* or *Lugh's Fair*. Though the name is traceable to the feast of an early sun-god named Lug or Lugh, the celebration has even more distant roots in an Egyptian festival connected to the cult of Isis. It is now Christianised and has become Lammas Day, possibly due to the 'lewd behaviour' that was said to take place in England, Ireland and the Isle of Man in former times during Lugnasad.

Lugh's Fair. See under Lugnassadh.

Luisech. 22 May. Irish female saint.

Luke (Evangelist). 18 October. Depicted with, or as, a winged bull with a book, painting or picture of the Virgin Mary. He is variously the patron saint of doctors, sculptors and goldsmiths. Historically he was said to have been born in Syria and was a physician (and perhaps a painter) by trade. He was not a Jew or a disciple of Christ, but did travel widely with St Paul. He is believed to have written both the Gospel according to St Luke and the Acts of the Apostles. He is said to have died, unmarried in Bithynia, aged 74.

Luke's Summer. A period of warm weather which often begins around St Luke's Day.

Lumeria. 9 April. Roman festival.

Luna, Festival of. 31 March. Roman festival dedicated to the moon.

Lunes Day. See under Lugnassadh.

Lupercalia. 15 February. Roman festival in honour of Faunus, also known as Luercus, the god of fertility and the countryside. A brotherhood known as the Luperci (Brothers of the Wolf) administered fertility rites in early times. The sexual connotations were dropped when the festival was Christianised by Gelasius who replaced it with the Candlemas or Purification of the Virgin celebrations around 494. Valentine's Day is also said to be directly evolved from Lupercalia.

Lustrum. A sacrificial celebration that took place in Roman-occupied areas following the five-year census. The five year period came to be called a lustrum.

M

Mabon. 21 September (Autumn equinox). See also Mabyn.

Mabyn. 21 September. Female Cornish Celtic saint. See also Mabon.

Mac Dara of Connemara. 16 July and 28 September. Irish patron saint of fishermen.

Macarius. 2 January. Patron saint of pastry cooks. An interesting legend says that whilst baking he was bit by a gnat. Having killed it, he served penance by sitting naked in a gnat-infested marsh for six months.

Macha of Killiney. 6 February. Irish saint.

Machonna. 12 November. Celtic.

Machutus (Bishop). See under Malo.

Maclou. See under Malo.

Madoc. Feast day unknown. The name is retained in a number of Welsh place-names.

Madron. 17 May. Cornish Celtic saint.

Maelog. See under Faelog.

Maelrhuba. Ancient patron of Applecross.

Magalesia. 4 to 10 April. Roman.

Magdalene, Mary. See under Mary Magdalene.

Maglore. 24 October.

Magnus. 19 August.

Magnus of Orkney. 16 April. An 11th century Earl of Orkney who became Orkney's patron saint. He was a pirate who was captured by Vikings. He joined them but refused to attack Britain. He returned to Orkney where he was killed in 1116 in a plot organised by his cousin, Haakon, the joint ruler of the island.

Mairead. 10 June. Scottish female saint.

Malachy of Armagh. 3 November. Irish saint.

Malo. 15 November. Patron saint of the town of St Malo. Though a saint of Brittany he was widely celebrated throughout Celtic Britain as he was a Welshman by birth. He is also known by the names of Machutus and Maclou. He served under St Brendon at Aleth monastery, in Brittany and became Bishop of Aleth himself. The town of St Malo now stands on the monastery site on the island of Aaron. He died 627.

Mamuralia. 14 March. A day dedicated to Mamurius during the month-long Roman festival of Feriae Marti.

Manacca. 14 October. Female Cornish Celtic saint.

Mandati. See Maundy Thursday.

Marcan of Clonenagh. 21 October. Irish saint.

Marcellus and Apuleius. 7 October.

Marcellinus and Peter. 2 June.

March Fast. 24 March.

Mardi Gras. Shrove Tuesday.

Maree. 25 August. Pagan sacrifice festival. See under Mourie.

Margaret (of Antioch). 20 July. She was the patron saint of maidens but in modern terms the patron saint of all women. She is also patron of nurses and peasant people everywhere. Her emblem is a dragon. Historically she is supposed to have been the daughter of a heathen priest of Antioch in Pisidia but was taught Christianity by her nurse. When her father found out, he expelled her from the household and she lived with the nurse, tending sheep for a living. The regional prefect, Olybius, who wanted to marry her, is said to have had her imprisoned when she said she was already married to Christ. She was tortured and beheaded for her beliefs in 304.

St Margaret of Antioch – Who is said to have appeared constantly to Joan of Arc.

Margaret (Queen). 8 July. St Margaret, former Queen of Scotland, died 1093. Her emblem is a black cross.

Marinus. 3 or 4 September. St Marinus' Day was little celebrated in England except under the influence of continental priests. He is the patron saint of San Marino (St Marinus) which was said to have been built upon his burial or death place.

Mark (Evangelist). 25 April. Said to be the disciple of Paul upon whose teachings he wrote the Gospel of St Mark in the Bible. He is synonymous with Markus and John Mark, cousin of St Barnabus and son of Mary, whose home was used as a Christian meeting place in Jerusalem. He was martyred in Alexandria whilst teaching the Christian gospel. He is said to have been dragged through the streets by the neck and to have died in prison shortly afterwards. His remains were taken to Venice in 829 and were placed in a vault beneath the altar of St Mark's Basilica. Depicted with (or as) a winged lion and a book, he is the patron saint of glaziers, notaries and of the City of Venice. See also Litania Major and Robigalia.

Mark and Marcellianus. 18 June.

Mark's Vigil. Held on St Mark's Eve (24 April) at churchyards when the watchers would supposedly see in the shadows the forms of all those who would die in the following year.

Marnoc. Feast day unknown. Celtic saint.

Mars. See under Feriae Marti.

Mars Ultor. 12 May. Roman festival dedicated to reconsecration of the Temple of Mars.

Martha. 29 July. The patron saint of housewives, innkeepers, cafe proprietors and all who cook food, as well as laundry workers. Often depicted with a dragon, which in German legends she is said to have slain using Holy water and her own girdle.

Martin. 11 November. Saint and former Bishop of Tours in France. He is patron saint of tavern keepers, wine growers and beggars. Historically he is known to have been born of Pagan parents in Sabaria (Pannonia) and was placed in the army as an officer aged 15 to try and dissuade him from becoming a Christian monk. He became a conscientious objector and refused to fight in the German war that had begun. After release from prison at the war's end he took up his religious calling and was eventually elected Bishop of Tours. He died 9 November 401 aged at least 80 years and was buried two days later. Martinmas was also called Martlemas and was the time when Martlemas beef, mutton and bacon were hung in the chimney to smoke, in order to provide meat during the coming winter months. See also under Beggars' Day.

Martin, Translation of. 4 July.

Martinmas. 11 November. See under Martin, above.

Martin's Lent. Six or seven Sundays beginning on St Martin's Day (11 November).

Martin's Summer A period of warm weather that often occurs around Martinmas.

Martlemas. See under Martin.

Mary (Virgin). See under Virgin Mary.

Mary of Egypt. 2 April.

Mary Magdalene. 22 July. Believed controversially by some to be the wife of Christ, by others a reformed prostitute. She is the woman mentioned in the Bible (Luke vii 30-50). She is depicted usually either with long hair and a jar of ointment, or as a virgin dressed in black. The name Magdalene is believed to indicate that she was from Magdala, near the Sea of Galilee. Some scholars believe she followed St John to Ephesus and it was she, not the Virgin Mary that retired there. It is interesting to note that the Virgin Mary's house and shrine in Ephesus depicts a black virgin to this day. Another tale tells how she, with Lazarus and Martha, possibly her brother and sister, took a boat to Marseilles in France where she lived for 30 years, some say, bringing up her child. A number of places, including the abbey of Vezelai, claim to hold her remains. See also under Joseph and Virgin Mary.

Mary Salome. 22 October.

Matralia. 11 June. Roman.

Matronalia. 1-7 March. Roman festival dedicated to Juno. With it commenced the Feriae Marti (Mars Fair).

Matthew (Evangelist). 21 September. Author of first Gospel in the Bible. Depicted usually as an angel holding a book or with a bag of money, as he is the patron saint of bankers and tax collectors. He is also called Levi and may have been either a publican or a customs official. Though some accounts say he died a natural death, it is believed he may have been slain by a sword in Ethiopia, where it is said he ended his days.

Mathias. 24 February (in a leap year, celebrated on 25 February). Apostle, patron saint of carpenters and tailors. Some records show him as being martyred in Ethiopia where he was preaching, whilst others say he was martyred in Jerusalem where he was stoned and then killed with an axe.

Matuta. 11 May. Roman festival.

Maughold. 31 January, also 27 April in the Isle of Man where he is patron saint. He was a 5th century pirate who converted to Christianity after landing safely on the island in an oarless boat.

Maundy Thursday. Thursday before Easter, commemorating the Last Supper of Christ. In England the Queen distributes special Maundy currency. The name is a corruption of the Latin, *dies mandati*, being the day of the mandate to love one another given by Christ whilst washing the feet of his disciples. It was also known in some areas as Green Thursday, an anglicised translation of its German counterpart.

Maurice (and others). 22 September. The 'others' often celebrated on this day were St Maurice's soldiers, who were, like Maurice, Christians in the army of the Theban Legion in which he served as an officer. The story is told how Maurice and his fellow Christians whilst fighting in Gaul, refused their Commander's orders when crossing the Alps. He had ordered them all to take part in Roman Pagan rites. They were all massacred for their refusal.

Mawe. 15 November.

Mawgan. 26 September. Cornish Celtic saint.

Mawlid An Nabi. Celebrated around 20 August. It commemorates the birth of Muhammad on 20 August 570 (12th Rabi'al-Awwal in Muslim calendar).

May Day. 1 May. Maypoles were once common all over England and were kept from one year to the next. These were usually tree trunks or long branches and did not always resemble the maypoles of modern times. The tallest maypole is said to have been erected in London on the Strand in 1661; it stood over 143 feet high. It was 'felled' in 1717, when it was used by Isaac Newton to support Huygen's new reflecting telescope. Belief that the ribbons and dances associated today with maypoles only date from the 1800s is false as the ribbons were carried on horses and carts (see Horse Ribbon Day) in the north of England from very early days. These would be paraded to the maypole to which they would be attached before dancing took place. Though today only the May Queen is elected during celebrations, it was once common also to elect a May King (known as the Green Man or Jack-a-Green). This is believed to have developed from the much earlier myth of Cybele and Attis and the Pagan practices surrounding it. See under Blood Days and Cybele (and Attis).

May Day – The London chimney sweeps' parade in the early 1800s featured a walking maypole bedecked in greenery accompanied by the Lord and Lady of the May leading a band of soot faced sweeps.

Left: May Day celebrations in Hitchin, Herts, around 1825. Right: Milkmaids parade in London on May Day around the same time.

May Eve. 30 April.

May Gosling Day. See under Gosling Day.

Meallan/ Maelrub(ha). 2 February and 26 October. Irish saint.

Medana. See under Triduana's Fast

Medard and Gildard. 8 June.

Meditrinalia. 11 October. Roman wine festival in honour of Medrita/Meditrina.

Megalesia. 10 April. Marks the end of the long Pagan festival of the Great Mother.

Megalesia to Cybele. See under Cybele (and Attis).

Melan. 6 January. Saint of Brittany widely celebrated throughout Celtic Britain.

Melitus. 24 April.

Mell Day. Moveable festival during harvesting, either when honey was collected or when Mell Cakes, a kind of scone with cinnamon and honey, were served at the end of the final day of the corn harvest.

Melle. 9 March. Female Celtic saint.

Melorius. 1 October.

Menna. 11 November.

Mens. 8 May. The Roman festival of wisdom and knowledge was a part of Lemuria. See under Lemuria.

Metonic Cycle. A period of 19 solar years or 235 moons when the phases of the moon turn to falling on the same days of the year. The dates of the full moon were inscribed in gold on public buildings in Greece and the number showing the position of the moon in that cycle is called the Golden Number. The discovery of the cycle was made by a Greek astronomer, Meton, in the year 432 BC. The Golden Number, used for determining moveable feasts, is calculated by adding 1 to the number of the year (AD) and dividing by 19. The result is the Golden Number unless the result is nil in which case it is 19.

Meven. 12 June. Saint of Brittany widely celebrated throughout Celtic Britain.

Mercury/Mercuralia. 15 May. Roman festival.

Meriadec. 7 June. Celtic saint of Brittany. Celebrated elsewhere and possibly same as the Cornish St Meryasek.

Meryasek. 7 June. Cornish Celtic saint. See also Meriadec.

Meryn. 6 January. Cornish saint.

Michael (and All Angels). 29 September. See under Michael (Archangel) below.

Michael, Apparition of. 8 May. Celebrates the apparition of the Archangel Michael. See below under Michael (Archangel).

Michael (Archangel). 29 September. Patron saint of artists, soldiers, police officers and grocers. He is often depicted trampling the devil or a dragon and to distinguish him from St George, who is also depicted killing a dragon, Michael carries a pair of scales with his sword. The Festival of Michaelmas celebrated on this day was traditionally accompanied by the killing and eating of geese and was one of the festivals particularly dear to rural communities. He is considered the supreme angel by Christians, Jews, followers of Islam and even in history, of the Chaldeans. His name means 'who is God' and he bears a 'secret name', *Sabbathiel*. Like St Peter, he also holds the keys to heaven in traditional belief systems.

Michael in Monte Tumba. 16 October.

Michaelmas. See under Michael (Archangel).

Michael (Micul) of the Isles. 21 September. Celtic saint, mainly celebrated in Scotland.

Michael's Day. 8 May. 'Pagan' Christian saint's day which developed from Furry Day.

Mid. See under Miz.

Midautumn Day. 21 September.

Mid-Lent Sunday. Also called Mothering Sunday and Latare Sunday. The fourth Sunday in Lent when worshippers are encouraged to visit their 'mother' church. See also Mothering Sunday.

Midsummer Bonfire Day. 23 June.

Midsummer's Day. 21 June (sometimes 23 June).

Midwinter's Day. 21 December.

Milburga. 23 February.

Mildred. 13 July.

Milyan. 6 November. Cornish Celtic saint.

Minor Litany. See under Litania Minor.

Mirren. 15 September. Scottish saint, patron of town of St Mirren.

Mithras. 25 December. Originally an Indo-European god, the cult of Mithras was probably brought to Britain by the Romans. He was known as 'The god of a thousand eyes and a thousand ears who embraces the universe'. In Indo-European beliefs he held sovereignty with Varuna whose 'qualities' were coercion and violence. Mithras, however, was her opposite and had the job of promoting harmony throughout the universe using non-hostility, good friendship and benevolence. Despite this he was patron saint of battles and held a place of judgment in Hell. In the *Avesta*, the 5th century holy book of Mazdaism, he was closely associated with the sun which he rode before, on a gold chariot pulled by two white horses. The Romans often depicted him as a bull slayer holding open the bull's nostrils whilst thrusting a sword into its side, with a dog, a snake and a scorpion close by. Mithras was also the god of salvation and as such could never die. The Rites of Mithras were often celebrated in caves with candidates having to complete seven levels of enlightenment, known as the Crow, the Griffin, the Soldier, the Lion, the Persian, the Courier and the Father. Each level had its own masks, duties and insignia. All ranks of Roman soldiers fell under the spell of Mithraism and temples were numerous within Britain and elsewhere. Statues of

Mithras – An ancient French illustration of a statue of Mithras as worshipped by the cult of Mithras in Britain and elsewhere. 'Mitra has borne the earth and sky for all time' (Rig Veda III,59,1).

Mithras came in a variety of forms, most either depicted the 1,000 eyes and ears or alternatively signs of the zodiac, indicating the god's universal status.

Mitra(s). See under Mithras.

Miz. Fourth Sunday before Easter Day. The Sundays before Easter were remembered by the rhyme 'Tid, Mid, Mizeray, Carling, Palm and Easter Day'. Mid probably means Mid-Lent, Miz may have connections with Miz Mazes, and Mizeray with ancient worship of the deity Mithras. See under that entry.

Mizeray. Third Sunday before Easter Day. See under Miz, above.

Mochuarog. Celtic Irish saint who founded Trinity Church (its modern name only) at Glendalough in the 7th century.

Modestus. See under Vitus.

Modwen. See under Osyth.

Modwenna. See under Triduana.

Moluag/Moluoc. 25 June. Northern Celtic saint who died in 592. Some of his relics survive on Lismore Island, at the entrance to Loch Linnhe, Scotland.

Monica. 4 May. Monica was the mother of St Augustine, Bishop of Hippo. She was of African birth, married Patricius, a Pagan and had two sons, Augustine and Navigius. She was herself a Pagan until late in life and followed Augustine to Milan, witnessing his baptism there by St Ambrose at Easter 387. Falling sick, she wished to return home, but died on the way at Ostia. She is often depicted in religious imagery dressed as a nun, holding hands with St Augustine.

Moninne of Killevy. 6 July. Female Irish saint.

Moon, Festival of the. 31 March. Roman festival.

Morgan(a/e). 8 October. Female Celtic saint.

Morrow of Christmas. 26 December.

Morwenna. 5 July. Female Cornish Celtic saint.

Mother Earth, Festival of. 15 April. Pagan festival that developed from the Roman festival of Terra Mater.

Mothering Sunday. Fourth Sunday in Lent. Also known as Laetare Sunday. It is traditionally the day in Britain when children gather (or buy) flowers for their mother. The day has its origin in Floralia (see under that entry) festivities and Pagan celebration of the 'earth-mother' and fertility. See also Mid-Lent Sunday.

Mother's Day. Commercialised version of Mothering Sunday. See under that entry.

Mother's Night. 24 December.

Mouree. 25 August. Celtic saint whose name may be taken from the Pagan sacrificial festival of Maree. It is known that bulls were still being sacrificed in Scotland on this day in 17th century Scotland.

Muaddnat of Drumcliffe. 6 January. Female Irish saint.

Muhammad. See under Mawlid An-Nabi.

Muna. Feast day uncertain. Irish saint venerated especially in County Wexford. He is said to have saved St Kevin from temptation by the Devil.

Mungo. 14 January. Also known as Kentigern (see under that entry).

Munnu. See under Fintan.

Myfor. Feast day unknown. Welsh.

N

Name of Jesus. 7 August.

Natalis Solis Invicti. See under Sol Invictus.

Nativity of John the Baptist. 24 June.

Nativity of Mary. See under Virgin Mary, Conception of.

Neck Festival. Harvest festival (southern Britain).

Nemesia. 23 August.

Nemo/Nemetonia. Moveable feast days. Nemo was a female goddess of slaughter and was associated with battle offerings and with the slaughter of white cattle when the mistletoe was gathered. Probably the same as Nerthus and with the festival of Nemoralia (see below).

Nemoralia. 13 August. Roman festival celebrated in woods and groves with lakes, in honour of the goddess Diana (*Diana Nemorensis* meaning Goddess of the Wood). See also under Nemo.

Neot. 13 July.

Neptunalia. 23 July. Roman maritime festival in honour of the sea-god Neptune.

Neptune. 23 September. Modern Pagan festival based on the discovery of the planet Neptune in the 19th century. A neo-Pagan revival of Elusinia. In ancient times the sea-god Neptune was believed to be the god of the common people (particularly seafarers). As such he did not like the higher or lower stratas of society and it was therefore considered bad luck to have a prostitute or a dignitary on board ship. Because of the need for dignitaries to be carried on ships, it was expected that they would throw something overboard as a sacrifice to ensure the ship's safe passage. A 17th century writer noted: '*...But thus superstition they still retain, that they will not endure a whore on shipboarde who they do believe causes storme and they will make bold to throw her overboard (as a sacrifice to Neptune). When the Morocco Ambassador came to England he was in a dangerous storme and he caused a ram to be sacrificed.*

The like opinion they have of a dead body on shipboarde which they hold to be very unlucky, and if a storme arises they will throw it into the sea as they did with that rare mummie that Sir Peter Wych brought from Egypt...'

Nereus and Achilleus. 12 May.

Nerthus. See under Nemo. She was associated with white cattle and the sacrifice of slaves by drowning.

Neven. 6 June. Celtic saint of Brittany, celebrated elsewhere.

New Fires. Pagan general name for the new Christianised versions of ancient Pagan fire festivals.

New Sunday. See under Low Sunday.

New Year's Day. 1 January. It was traditional in the north of England to celebrate New Years's Day more than Christmas. Christmas was considered a religious festival, whilst the New Year festival was considered one of pleasure. It relates to the Scottish Hogmanay, and often involves a 'first footer' passing over the threshold as soon as possible after the last strike of the clock on New Year's Eve. This 'first footer' was traditionally a male, sound in health with dark hair. Tradition varied from area to area, but often the man would be a stranger carrying a piece of coal. It was believed that the ceremony would bring good luck to the household for the rest of the year. Ancient Hogmanay festivities used to involve a man dressed as a bull who would run clockwise around each villager's house before entering and burning bull's hair in the fire, whilst wishing the occupiers health, wealth and the same for their cattle. Games and revelling would follow. It was anciently also called Hogmagog (Hogmanay) or the festival of Gog and Magog or Gogmagog, Gog being associated with the sun and Magog with the moon.

New Year's Eve. 31 December (modern calendar). It was traditional in the north on New Year's Eve for even the youngest children to stay up until midnight when they would go around in groups, knocking on the doors of any house with a light on, and wishing the occupants 'Happy New Year', for which in return they would receive money. Though some gave to more than one group of callers, others did not. The practice, though still surviving, largely died out in the late 1960s when parents, fearing for the safety of their unaccompanied children, refused to let them out at such a late hour.

Newlyn(a). 27 April. Female Cornish Celtic saint.

Neythen. 17 June. Cornish Celtic saint.

Nicholas (Bishop of Myra). 6 December. Died 326 (or 350). He is the patron saint of all children and is depicted as Santa Claus or Father Christmas, though the character of Santa Claus is relatively new to Britain having been imported from America. In 1827 the Santa Claus tradition was described by an English writer as 'unknown with us'. In early Europe it was traditional for people to leave gifts for others without saying who they were from on St Nicholas' Eve (5 December). This was said to have been started by St Nicholas (also known as Klaus, Klaas etc) when he was Bishop of Myra in Lycia. The custom later spread to America via Dutch immigrants. Though originally dressed all in white, his costume in modern western Europe is depicted as red. He is also the patron saint of all prisoners and of travellers, merchants and those overtaken by sudden distress or danger. His emblem is three balls, indicative of the gold he so freely gave away as a rich man. Pawnbrokers adopted his symbol. He is also portrayed by three children in a tub. Though he died and was buried at Myra in 326, his remains were translated to Bari on the Italian coastline in 1084.

Nicholas, Translation of. 9 May.

Nicodemus. 4 August

Nicomede the Martyr. 1 June. Said to have been beaten to death in Rome, with leaded whips, having been found burying the corpse of a Christian martyr.

Nigasius. 6 October.

Night of the Mothers. 24 December.

Night of the Wild Hunt. Eve of 1 November.

Night Watches. See under Easter Vigil.

Nile Day. 15 June.

Ninian. 16 September. British born pre-Saxon saint who was educated at Bangor. According to Bede he went to Rome where he stayed before returning to Britain to help convert the Picts to Christianity. He built a Christian church at Candidam Casam (Kirkudbright), became its bishop and died there. His visit to Rome is disputed by some scholars.

Ninth Day (before Christmas). 16 December. Start of the Christmas period for some Roman Catholics. The days between the 16th and 24th represent each of the months of the Virgin Mary's confinement.

Nolwen. 6 July. Female Celtic saint.

Nonae Caprotinae. 7 July. Roman festival dedicated to Juno which ran into the festival of Juno the following day.

Nones. The seventh day of the months of March, May, July and October and the fifth day of the other months (ninth day before the ides).

Nonna. 2 March. Female Cornish Celtic saint.

November Eve. Another name for Samhain.

November Fast. 29 November.

Nutcrack Night. See under Samhain.

O

O Sapienta. 16 December.

Oak Apple Day. 29 May. Celebrated after the restoration to the throne of King Charles II to commemorate the battle of Worcester. To escape his enemies, Charles had to hide in an oak tree and the oak apple (oak gall) became a symbol of his deliverance. Also known as Royal Oak Day.

Oak Festival. 21 June. Midsummer's day.

Oak King. Ancient festival held at the Summer Solstice. A similar winter festival of the Holly King was also held to celebrate mid-winter's day.

October Fasts. 27 and 31 October.

Odilo. 1 January. He is said to have been the person who created the Christian All Souls' Day from a Pagan festival.

Odo. 2 June.

Odran. 8 May. Irish saint who is patron saint of Waterford. Possibly the saint who was commemorated on the Isle of Man on 27 February, the same date as the festival of St Oran in the Scottish Isles.

Oengus Ceile De. 11 March. Irish saint also called Angus and Aonghus.

Oestra. See under Ostara.

Oimelc. 1 February. One of the Four Great Fire Festivals (see under that entry). An important, though the least significant of the four main fire festivals, it was the first to disappear (though not completely). Lenten Fires became a Christianised way of celebrating the feast. Other versions of this festival are St Bridget's Day, Candlemas and St Blaise's Day (1, 2 and 3 of February, respectively).

Oissine. 1 January, also 1 May. Irish saint.

Olaf. 29 July. Scandinavian saint, celebrated throughout northern Britain and Ireland. He was King of Norway between the years 1016 and 1029 and was exiled and killed at the Battle of Stiklestad in 1030 without regaining his throne.

Olaille. 12 February.

Opalia. 19 December, also 9 and 13 December. Roman festivals dedicated to Ops (see below).

Opec(onsiva)/Opiconsivia. 25 August. Roman festival.

Opiconsivia. 25 December. Roman festival dedicated to Ops (see below).

Ops. 10 August. Roman festival dedicated to the celebration of might and power.

Oraea. 21 June. Roman festival.

Oran. 27 February. Oran was said to have been buried alive under the foundations of St Columban's monastery in order to appease the spirits of the soil that demolished buildings. See also under Odran.

Orange Day. See Orangeman's Day (below).

Orangeman's Day. 12 July. Also called Orange Day. Irish holiday celebrating Protestant victory over the Catholics at the Battle of the Boyne in 1690.

Orion. 10 and 11 May. Roman festival dedicated to Orion.

Orthodoxy Sunday. Another name for Quadragesima. See under that entry.

Osith. 7 October.

Osmund. 4 December. Osmund arrived in Britain after the Battle of Hastings from Normandy, where he was of noble birth. He was Royal Chaplain and later Chancellor (1067). In 1087 he became Bishop of Salisbury at the new cathedral at Old Sarum. He was thought to have initiated the Saturn Rite, based on Roman practices. Osmund is said to have worked on the draft of the Domesday Book. He died in 1099 and was buried at Old Sarum but his remains were moved to the new cathedral of Salisbury in 1226. It took 228 years from the original moves to make him a saint to his actual canonisation in 1456 by Pope Calistus III.

Osmund, Translation of. 16 July.

Ostara. The Vernal or Spring Equinox (see under that entry). Ostara was a Norse maiden goddess of fertility. Her emblems were a seed, an egg and a rabbit, all symbols of fecundity. In Pagan culture this was the start of the season of planting seeds. The name Easter is derived from Ostara who was also known as Oestra/Eostra and gave her name to oestrogen, the female fertility hormone.

Oswald (Bishop). 28 February. Served his early years as a Cluniac monk in Fleury, France.

Oswald (King). 5 August. Prince Oswald was the son of Northumbrian King Ethelrith and fled to Iona from Scotland when his father lost his throne, becoming a Christian there. He is noted for killing the tyrant Cadwalla in battle, so becoming a king himself. One of his first acts was to attempt to Christianise Britain and he gave Lindisfarne to (St) Aiden to form a Bishopric. Having united Bernicia and Deira, the two halves of Northumbria, he married the Wessex princess, Cynegils. Oswald was killed (aged 38) by King Penda in 642 at the Battle of Maserfield (Shropshire). Oswald's body was mutilated and dismembered. Later the parts of his body began appearing in churches throughout Britain and even abroad where miracles were attributed to their presence. He is venerated throughout Britain, and in European countries as far apart as Portugal and Austria. See also Rush Bearing Day.

Oswin. Date uncertain. Holy King and Martyr whose discovered body led to the rebuilding of Tynemouth Priory. The northern saint's book is held in the British Museum.

Osyth. 7 August. Celebrated widely in Essex in earlier times. She was the daughter of Redwald (or Frithwald) and Wilburga, King and Queen of the East Angles. She is said to have drowned, after trying to deliver a book from St Edith (sister of King Alfred), only to be revived by St Modwen. She was beheaded in October 653 by the Danes when she refused to give up her Christian religion.

Our Lady of Mount Carmel. 16 July.

Our Lady of Perpetual Help. 27 June.

Our Lady of Sorrow. See under Virgin Mary.

Our Lady of the Angels. 2 August.

Our Lady of the Snow. 5 August.

Our Lady's Presentation at Temple. 21 November.

Our Lady... See also under Virgin Mary.

Owen. 24 or 25 August.

P

Pachomius. Date uncertain. Pachomius was instrumental in helping to form the early Christian monastic movement.

Padarn. Possibly a moveable feast day, often held in April. Known in Wales as Badarn.

Padraig. Irish name for St Patrick (Bishop and Saint). See under that entry.

Padrig. Name used in Brittany for St Patrick (Bishop and Saint). See under that entry.

Paganalia. 24, 25, 26 January. Also known as Sementivae (Roman).

Palilia. 21 April. Roman festival of purification dedicated to the god Pallas when farm animals were driven through burning straw to cleanse them of the insects which had infested them during their winter indoor habitation.

Palm Saturday. The day before Palm Sunday when it was traditional to gather willow branches, which were used to decorate houses and churches.

Palm Sunday. First Sunday before Easter Day, commemorating Christ entering Jerusalem. The day of the Battle of Towton (Tadcaster, Yorkshire) was known as Sad Palm Sunday as it fell on Palm Sunday, 29 March 1463 (Wars of the Roses).

Pancake Day. Shrove Tuesday when pancakes were (and are) eaten, to use up ingredients prior to the fast of Lent. The first, usually imperfect, pancake was generally given to ugly women as a charm to make them more beautiful. Naturally no woman in an ordinary household would eat the first pancake and so it was fed to the family dog.

Pancras. 12 May. Known to most British people as the saint commemorated in the name of a London railway station, St Pancras was a Phrygian of noble birth. His uncle was Dionysus, who brought him to Rome on the death of Pancras's father to be baptised. It was in Rome that he was martyred for his faith. The first church built in Canterbury by St Augustine was dedicated to St Pancras, who is said to be a sworn enemy of those who tell untruths. He died circa 304 and is often depicted holding a palm branch.

Papist Conspiracy – An excellent example of how a Pagan festival developed into a Church festival which in turn became our modern Guy Fawkes Night or Gunpowder Plot. The above illustration is from a 19th-century wood-cut engraving showing boys transporting a Guy through the streets.

Papist Conspiracy. 5 November. Celebrated in 18th century churches as a day of thanksgiving against the Papist Conspiracy when Guy Fawkes and his conspirators tried to blow up the Houses of Parliament. It is now celebrated as Gunpowder Plot or Guy Fawkes Night with the burning of bonfires and the letting off of fireworks. Again it represents the Christianisation of a Pagan festival, namely the Celtic Samhain, and like Hallowe'en has even earlier links with Pagan festivals. See also under Samhain.

Parentalia. 13 to 21 February. Roman festival.

Paschal Day. Good Friday.

Paschal Week. See under Holy Week.

Passion Sunday. Fifth Sunday in Lent. Also known as Judica and Carling Sunday. See under Carling Sunday.

Passion Week. See under Holy Week.

Passiontide. Period of religious celebration from Passion Sunday to Holy Saturday.

Passover. Jewish festival.

Paste Egg Day. Easter Monday (or Sunday) when children in some areas would celebrate by rolling eggs down hills.

Pater Patria. 5 February. Also known as the Roman festival of Augustus, celebrating Augustus receiving the Pater Patria.

Patrick (Bishop and Saint). 17 March. Died 461 or 463. Patron saint of Ireland with the shamrock as his emblem. Often depicted in his bishop's robes accompanied by serpents. Patrick was said to have been born in Britain, captured by the Celts and taken to Ireland as a slave. Age 17, he escaped, trained as a monk and then went back to Ireland where he maintained a literary tradition during the Dark Ages. Known in Ireland as Padraig and in Brittany as Padrig.

Paul (Apostle). 13 June, also 30 June. Died AD c.64. His emblems are a sword and a book. He is the patron saint of missionaries and is well documented elsewhere.

Paul, Commemoration. 30 June.

Paul, Conversion of. 25 January. Said to be a festival when the future weather and fortunes of the nation could easily be predicted for the coming year. See also Ananius of Damascus.

St Paul – Preaching at Athens.

If Paul's Day be fair and clear, it does betide a lovely year
But if it chance to snow or rain, then shortages of oats and grain
If clouds or mist darken the sky, then many birds and beasts will die

And if the wind doth fly aloft, then war shall vex the kingdom oft.

Paul, Shipwreck of. 10 February.

Paulinus. 10 October. He was consecrated Bishop of York in 625 before accompanying Ethelburga, daughter of King Ethelbert, to Northumbria where he attempted to convert the Pagans to Christianity. He is said to have baptised 30,000 in one day at a well near Hepple, now called Holy Well. He also travelled widely in Yorkshire and Lincolnshire. After the battle of Heathfield, he fled with the widowed Ethelburga to Kent. He rebuilt the church at Glastonbury and was appointed to the see of Rochester where he died on 10 October 644.

Paum. Another name for Palm Sunday (see under that entry).

Pax. 4 July. Anciently in Roman times, the first day of Compitalia (1 to 5 January) was also known as the Festival of Pax.

Peadar. 4 June. Irish.

Peaste. Another name for Easter Monday.

Pedrog. 4 June. Cornish Celtic saint.

Pentecost. (See under Whit Sunday)

Pentecost Vigil See under Easter Vigil.

Perpetua (Martyr). 7 March. She was martyred at Carthage during the reign of Emperor Severus in 203 despite being implored by her Pagan father to renounce Christianity. Her death was in the arena, having been gored by a cow and finally being killed by a swordsman. She is said to have had a premonition of her martyrdom when dreaming of a ladder hung with knives and swords which was guarded by a dragon.

Peter ad Vincula. 1 August. Commemorates the day when St Peter, fleeing for his life from Rome, is supposed to have met Christ. Peter asked him where he was going and he replied that he was going to Rome to be crucified again. Peter, overcome by shame, is said to have returned to Rome to meet his fate. See also under Peter, Lammas, and Gule of August.

Peter and Paul. 29 June. See also Peter ad Vincula.

Peter (Apostle). 29 June. Shown wearing a papal tiara and carrying a bunch of keys, he is traditionally the guardian of heaven's gates. He is also the patron saint of butchers, bakers and clockmakers. See also Lammas Day. Tradition states that every church dedicated to St Peter should have a church dedicated to St John nearby, though this is not always the case. St Peter's Eve was traditionally marked by the lighting of bonfires and burning of rows of tar barrels in the streets. The name of Peter (Cephas, Kephas or Petros, meaning Rock) was given to him during his missionary work, though he was born Simon or Simeon, the brother of St Andrew. He died by crucifixion in Rome but by his own request was crucified upside down so as not to imitate the crucifixion of Christ. His body was buried in Rome near the Tri-

St Peter – Shown during his lifetime when an angel is said to have visited him in prison.

umphal Way before being taken to a cemetery of the Appenine Way. Pope Cornelius finally brought his body back to Rome to be buried in the church of St Peter.

Peter, Chair of. 22 February.

Petroc. See under Kevin.

Philip. 1 May. 1st century Apostle and Martyr. He accompanied Christ and was martyred at Hierapolis, Phrygia after destroying the heresy of the Elionites. At the advanced age of 87, he was buried, according to Polycrates, Bishop of Ephesus, at Heirapolis with his two virgin daughters, another daughter being buried in Ephesus where the Virgin Mary is believed by some to have ended her days. See also under Virgin Mary and James the Lesser.

Philip and James. 1 May. See also under James the Less(er).

Pigrimage to Purgatory. 1 June. Traditionally the day St Patrick opened the earth to give the Irish a view of hell and its demons.

Celebrated by a pilgrimage on this day to St Patrick's Cave on an island in Lough Derg.

Piran. 5 March. Cornish saint.

Plebeian Games. 4 to 17 November. The same as Plebii.

Plebii. 4 to 17 November. Roman festival celebrated by the common people.

Pleiades. 2 April. Roman festival dedicated to Pleiades. The rising of the seven stars in that constellation indicated a safe time to sail on long voyages.

Plough Monday. Monday after 6 January when 'Plough Stots' and 'Sword Dancers' would dance. A full detailed account of sword dancing, plough festivals and similar festivals, including the traditional names of characters taking part, can be found in *Whitby Lore and Legend* (1923 edition) by Shaw Jefferey. See also under Epiphany for main description, and under Stephen Protomartyr.

Pol. 12 March. Celtic saint of Brittany, celebrated elsewhere.

Polycarp. 26 January. A bishop of Smyrna who was one of the 'Apostolic Fathers', Polycarp was a disciple of St John the Evangelist. He died at the stake in 166 (some records state 155), refusing to denounce Christ. He is accepted by many as the very first 'saint' of Christianity whose life was remembered on a set day each year. A legend tells that his burning body smelled of incense and that when Polycarp's side was pierced with a spear, a dove appeared and quenched the flames, that were burning around him, with his blood.

Poplifugia. 5 July. Roman festival dedicated to Jupiter.

Portunalia. 17 August. Roman festival dedicated to Portunes.

Poseidon. 1 December. Roman and Pagan festival.

Presentation of Christ in the Temple. 2 February (15 February in Old Style calendar).

Presentation of Our Lady at the Temple. See under Our Lady.

Primrose Day. 19 April. Celebrated in memory of the death of Lord Beaconsfield. The Primrose League was formed in 1883 to promote his political principles and the emblem of a primrose was worn on Primrose Day.

Prisca (Virgin and Martyr). 18 January. Martyred because she refused to denounce Christ. She was said to have been beheaded at the age of 13 having survived being thrown to

Plough Monday

The first *Monday* after Twelfth-day is called *Plough* Monday, and appears to have received that name because it was the first day after Christmas that husbandmen resumed the *plough*. In some parts of the country, and especially in the north, they draw the plough in procession to the doors of the villagers and townspeople. Long ropes are attached to it, and thirty or forty men, stripped to their clean white shirts, but protected from the weather by waistcoats beneath, drag it along. Their arms and shoulders are decorated with gay-coloured ribbons, tied in large knots and bows, and their hats are smartened in the same way. They are usually accompanied by an old woman, or a boy dressed up to represent one; she is gaily bedizened, and called the *Bessy*. Sometimes the sport is assisted by a humorous countryman to represent a *fool*. He is covered with ribbons, and attired in skins, with a depending tail, and carries a box to collect money from the spectators. They are attended by music, and Morris-dancers when they can be got; but there is always a sportive dance with a few lasses in all their finery, and a superabundance of ribbons. When this merriment is well managed, it is very pleasing. The money collected is spent at night in conviviality. It must not be supposed, however, that in these times, the twelve days of Christmas are devoted to pastime, although the custom remains. Formerly, indeed, little was done in the field at this season, and according to "Tusser Redivivus," during the Christmas holidays, gentlemen feasted the farmers, and every farmer feasted his servants and taskmen. Then *Plough Monday* reminded them of their business, and on the morning of that day, the men and maids strove who should show their readiness to commence the labours of the year, by rising the earliest. If the ploughman could get his whip, his plough-staff, hatchet, or any field implement, by the fireside, before the maid could get her kettle on, she lost her Shrove-tide cock to the men. Thus did our forefathers strive to allure youth to their duty, and provided them innocent mirth as well as labour. On Plough Monday night the farmer gave them a good supper and strong ale. In some places, where the ploughman went to work on Plough Monday, if, on his return at night, he came with his whip to the kitchen-hatch, and cried "Cock in pot," before the maid could cry "Cock on the dunghill," he gained a cock for Shrove Tuesday.

the lions, her body protected by an eagle until Christians arrived to take it away.

Priscus. 1 September.

Prosperine. 26 May to 30 June. The festival of Prosperine continued through the festival of Diana but extended until 30 June. See under Diana.

Purification of the Virgin. 2nd February. See also Lupercalia from which it is said to have evolved.

Purification of Trumpets. See under Tubilustrium.

Purim. Jewish festival also called the Feast or Festival of Lots and celebrated on 14th Adar, four weeks before Passover. Celebrated with religious readings.

Q

Quadragesima. First Sunday in Lent. Also used to describe the forty-day fast of Lent.

Quarter Days. These are listed in various ways by different authorities, including (a) the Feast of the Nativity of the Virgin Mary, the Annunciation, St John the Baptist and St Michael (churches in England and Wales only); (b) Lady Day, Midsummer Day, Michaelmas and Christmas (civil); (c) Whitsun, Martinmas, Candlemas and Lammas (known as Term Days in Scotland).

Quasimodo Sunday. See under Easter Octave.

Queenship of Virgin Mary. 31 May. Equates to Mother's Day.

Quinquagesima. See under Shrove Sunday.

Quinquatrus. 19 to 21 or 24 March, 13 May and 13 June. Roman festival dedicated to Minerva and to Mars.

Quinquatrus Minusculoe. 13 June. Roman.

Quirinalia. 17 February. Roman festival dedicated to Quirilinus.

R

Raksha Bandhan. Celebrated by the Indian community in general though it is principally a Hindu festivity. Sikhs give rakhi bracelets made of shiny and glittering materials together with greeting cards.

Ramadan. Moveable feast in the ninth month of the Mohammedan calendar. Equivalent to Lent. A fast begins before dawn and ends at dusk. See also Eid-Ul-Fitr.

Raphael (Archangel). 24 October. His emblems are the gall of a fish and a jar of ointment. He is the patron saint of all guardian angels and as such is believed to be the guardian of all souls and to have the power of healing.

Rebirth (of the sun). 21 December. Midwinter's Day.

Red Letter Day. Any saint's day, so called because the dates were marked in red on old calendars.

Reek Sunday. Last Sunday in July. Also known as Smoke Sunday.

Refreshment Sunday. See under Laetare Sunday.

Regifugium. 24 February. Roman festival of pomp and ceremony. It commemorated the expulsion of Tarquin.

Regulus. Often celebrated on St Andrew's Day because it was St Regulus who is credited with taking the bones of St Andrew to Scotland from Greece in defiance of an order by Emperor Constantine to take them to Constantinople (Istanbul). Regulus was also known as Rule.

Rejoicing Day (Sunday). Laetare Sunday.

Rejoicing of the Law. Jewish celebration.

Remembrance Sunday. Nearest Sunday to 11 November when the dead of all British wars are remembered at 11 am (being the eleventh hour of the eleventh day of the eleventh month). Also known as Armistice Day, especially just after World War I.

Remigius. 1 October or 13 January. This Archbishop of Reims, France was born at Laon and died 530. He became Archbishop at only 22 years and later baptised the Frank King Clovis, together with 3,000 others, into Christianity, in a single ceremony. He was said to have had a Jewish appearance, with a thick, tawny beard and a long, hooked nose and to be seven feet in height. His remains are in St Remi abbey, Reims.

Removal Terms. 28 May and 28 November. (Scotland).

Rewan. 30 August. Cornish Celtic saint.

Rex Comitiavit. 24 March. Conclusion of the month-long Feriae Marti dedicated to Mars. Rex Comitiavit means 'election of the king'. Also 24 May.

Rhidian. Feast day unknown. Welsh.

Richard (Bishop). 3 April. Richard of Wych (Droitwich), c.1197-1253, was a former bishop of Chichester. He is depicted in religious icons with a halo, driving a coach with four horses. In Milan, he was declared the patron of coachmen. Though coming from a well-to-do family, he entered the priesthood relatively late in life, rather than take the opportunity to marry a woman of means. Having travelled the world, he became Vicar of Deal and Rector of Charing. His election in 1244 as Bishop of Chichester did not meet with the approval of Henry II whose own candidate, Richard Passelew was rejected by the bishops. Despite being recognised as Bishop by the Pope, the King's opposition left Richard without a base and he travelled the south country, preaching for a crusade and, it is said, fishing for a living. He died on 3 April 1253 and was buried at Chichester Cathedral. A 'Guild of St Richard' existed at Eastbourne in the 15th century and his festival was kept as late as 1680. Wakes were held in his name even in the 1800s.

Riok. 12 February. Celtic saint of Brittany. Celebrated elsewhere.

Rising Nile Day. 15 June. Pagan.

Rites of Spring. See under Spring Equinox.

Robert (of Knaresborough). 24 September. He was born in York in 1160 and was possibly the son of a wealthy merchant of that city. Having served as a novice at Newminster abbey he moved to Knaresborough as a hermit, originally sharing a cave with a fugitive knight who was avoiding Richard I. He was later accused of harbouring outlaws and thieves by William de Stuteville, constable of Knaresborough and his hermitage was destroyed. However, later, when Robert was sponsored by King John, Stuteville gave him land and cattle and he gained a reputation for assisting the poor. Despite refusing to join the monks at Fountains Abbey before he died, Robert gained great respect from the religious community. His body was buried at his chapel near his original cave in Knaresborough where a chapel was later built on instructions of the Pope.

Robigalia. 25 April. This is the Roman festival mentioned by Sir James Frazer in his book *The Golden Bough*, where red haired puppies were sacrificed to avert the supposed blighting influence on the crops of the Dog Star.

Rock Day. 7 January. The end of the traditional Christmas holiday when women returned to their spinning. Also known as Distaff Day. The distaff was otherwise known as a rock.

Rogation Days. Monday, Tuesday and Wednesday before Holy Thursday (Ascension).

Rogation Sunday. The Sunday before the start of the Rogation Days (see above). It was often used as a time to bless crops or 'beat the bounds' and so mark the town or local landowner's boundaries. Both ceremonies were processional in nature and are believed to have evolved from earlier pre-Christian processional festivals, paricularly Ambarvalia. See under Litania Minor.

Roman Indication. Fiscal period of 15 years instituted by the Romans, c.300.

Romani. 15 to 19 September. Roman festival celebrated in countries occupied by the Roman forces.

Romuald. 7 February. Little is known of him other than that he was a desert hermit who earlier had retreated to a Benedictine monastery after witnessing the death of his father in a duel.

Ronan/Ronain. 7 February (in Scotland) and 1 June (in Brittany). A Celtic saint.

Ronan of Lismore. 9 February. Irish.

Rood Day. 1 May (also listed as 3 May and 7 May). Possibly a moveable feast. Also called Roodmas and The Invention of the Holy Cross.

Roodmas. 1 May.

Roparzh. 24 February. Celtic saint of Brittany. Celebrated elsewhere.

Rose Monday. Another name for Shrove Monday. See under that entry.

Rose Sunday. The fourth Sunday in Lent when anciently the Pope blessed a golden rose and sent it to a distinguished person. One such rose is preserved in the Musee de Cluny in

Paris. This celebration was described as 'ancient' even in 1049.

Rosh Hoshana. Jewish New Year.

Royal Oak Day. See under Oak Apple Day.

Ruadan. 15 April. Irish saint and former abbot of Lorrha.

Rule. See under Regulus.

Rush Bearing Day. The nearest Saturday to 5 August. Once celebrated throughout the north, if not all of England, now confined to the Lake District. See also under Oswald.

Ruth. Feast day unknown. Associated with Redruth, Cornwall. She has legendary mystical links with Glastonbury and the Christ-child coming to England. A belief was commonly held in folklore that Redruth was named after St Ruth, who came to the area wearing a red cloak.

S

Sabbat(h). In the Christian church, Sunday. In the Jewish belief, Saturday.

Sabbatum in Albis. See under Low Sunday.

Sacred Heart of Jesus. 31 August. It was instigated as a religious celebration on 31 August 1670 by Sir John Eudes, (1601-1680), a Frenchman educated as a Jesuit and who later joined the Oratorians (Congregation of the Oratory), undertaking the care of plague victims and later prostitutes.

Sad Palm Sunday. See under Palm Sunday.

Saf. See under Hermes.

Salus. 30 March. Roman festival.

Samhain. 1 November (eve of 31 October – Pagan pivotal point of the unstable spiritual world). It was one of the Four Great Fire Festivals of the Celts (see under that entry also) and corresponded to the Greek Chalceia, an ancient festival in

An old engraving showing family activities on Samhain Eve, also known as 'Nutcrack Night'.

honour of Hephaestus, and also with the Egyptian festival known as The Great Feast of the Dead which commemorated the slaying of Isis. It is easy to see why our Hallowe'en festival and our 5 November Bonfire Night are so close together as both correspond closely with these ancient festivals. To the Celts, fire which was propagated from another fire was considered to have lost its sacred properties. This is why at Samhain, all fires had to be extinguished and a new fire was made by friction. This *forced-fire* or *teine-eigin/tin-egin* was often kindled by the priesthood or the 'wise folk' of the neighbourhood after which all and sundry were allowed to carry burning embers to their own household fires. A Teutonic equivalent called *Neif Fyre* or *Not-Fyr* was known elsewhere than Britain. Though not strictly 'fire worship' as it is so often named, the Samhain ceremony was felt to have genuine mystical and religious significance and was carried out in Westmorland right up until the early 1900s, including the driving of cattle through the smoke of a fire produced by nut-wood (as in *Not-Fyre*). Even in France there is recorded an instance in 1879 when in the time-honoured tradition, a virgin was chosen to light the annual village fire whilst the oldest man in the village recited the *prayer of fire*. Strangely, the village priest was specifically excluded from taking any part in the ceremony. Samhain Eve was known as 'Nutcrack Night' in some areas and families would gather together to bob for apples and eat nuts.

Santo Stefano. See under Stephen Protomartyr.

Sapienta. 16 December.

Saturn Day. 26 December.

Saturnalia. 17 to 23 December. Roman festival to honour the god Saturn at the end of the harvest of the grapes (Saturnus was the god of agriculture). A feature of the festival was that slaves were waited upon by their masters and all class distinctions were ignored.

Seanan. See under Senan of Iniscathy.

Sebastian (Martyr). 20 January. Died 288 (or 303?). Sebastian was a Roman soldier of rank who survived a death sentence (shooting by arrows) imposed by Emperor Diocletian and returned to kill him, only to be arrested again and beaten to death. He is often depicted as being pierced by arrows. If not, then carrying one or more arrows. He is the patron saint of arms manufacturers, dealers, archers, athletes, ironmongers and potters and is said to protect all who venerate him, from the plague.

Secaire. Date unknown. A medieval saint whose mass became a sacrilegious feast. Any priest found celebrating his day was liable to excommunication.

Sementivae. 24, 25, 26 January. Also known as Paganalia. Roman.

Scholastica. 10 February. She was the sister of St Benedict and was abbess of a convent near Monte Cassino. She died in 548.

Seleven. 14 October. Cornish Celtic saint.

Sementivae. 13 December. Roman festival dedicated to Tellus.

Semo Sanctus. Roman festival held in June.

Senan of Iniscathy. 8 March. Irish saint.

September Fast. 20 September.

Septuagesima. The Sunday before Lent in Shrovetide. Also used to describe all three Sundays before Lent.

Serapis Mysteries. 6 May.

Serf/Serif/Serv. 6 May. Celtic.

Servan. See under Kentigern.

Seshat. See under Hermes.

Setsamhain. 1 May.

Seva. 23 July. Female Celtic saint.

Sexagesima. The second Sunday before Lent in Shrovetide.

Shavuot. Jewish feast of Pentecost.

Shone/Shonee/Shony Day. 1 November. Pagan sacrificial ceremony of blessing the boats, probably by the sprinkling of blood upon the sea. Records show that on the Scottish Isle of Lewis, ale was thrown into the sea on this date following the Christianisation of the community.

Shrove Monday. Monday before Ash Wednesday. Also called Rose Monday and Collop Monday.

Shrove Sunday. Sunday before Ash Wednesday. Also called Quinquagesima.

Shrovetide. The period when it was traditional for the English to confess their sins to the parish priest (to shrive means to confess). Traditionally celebrated in Ashbourne, Derbyshire and in Chester le Street on Shrove Tuesday as a football match

Shrove Tuesday – The two illustrations above show a once common way of celebrating Shrove Tuesday, known as 'threshing the hen'. Originally as shown left, it involved a cruel ceremony involving the brutal killing of hens which had ceased to lay. Later the 'hen' became a young farm-worker dressed in a costume with bells attached. Other young lads in blindfolds would chase him around the farmyard or village with flails until the 'hen' was eventually caught and a prize was won.

by all residents across the town and surrounding countryside. The football chase is probably a reminder of earlier ceremonies when a man would be chased until caught. This is evident in other areas where they celebrated Shrovetide with effigies of a straw man being burnt, or a 'green man' being ritually slaughtered. In reality it is believed that the ritual 'slaughter' was played out in the form still found in some areas in the early 1900s when a local man would run around with pigs' bladders filled with pigs' blood beneath his clothing. When captured he would be thrown to the ground (the 'sacrifice') upon which the bladders would burst. It was believed anciently that the blood would mystically regenerate the corn. Today we are aware that this is true, though modern farmers use 'blood and bone' fertiliser for the same purpose. In other places such as Ludlow, tug of war contests were the traditional way of celebrating Shrovetide.

Shrove Tuesday. The day after Shrove Monday.

Shushan Purim. Jewish festival.

Silvester. See under Sylvester.

Silyen. 29 July. Cornish Celtic patron saint of Luxulyan.

Simchat Torah. See under Succot(h).

Simon and Jude. 28 October. Christianised version of festival of Zetesis. It was a tradition that the Lord Mayor of London would be elected on this feast day and that he would be presented to the King and the Barons of the Exchequer on the next day (unless it was a Sunday). See also under Simon Zelotes (below) and under Lord Mayor's Day.

Simon (Archbishop). 14 June. Simon, Archbishop of Canterbury was martyred on 14 June 1381 when he was executed during the Peasants Revolt. Gruesome details tell us that the axeman John Starling struck eight blows before completing his task.

Simon Stylites. 5 January. Born at Gesa, between Antioch and Cilicia, this former shepherd boy left home and begged entry to a local monastery, where he exhibited a religious fervour that startled all of the monks. His unpopularity led to him becoming a hermit and he began a solitary life atop a large pillar on a mountainside from where he preached to gathering flocks of pilgrims and eventually died.

Simon Zelotes (the Canaanite). 28 October. Historically Simon was a 1st century Zealot who preached in Edessa and died

St Simon Stylites – A Victorian sketch of St Simon on his pillar.

a natural death, according to Eastern beliefs. However, in the West he is said to have preached in Persia and was martyred, either by crucifixion or by being sawn in half. Jude is also jointly celebrated on his day (see above, Simon and Jude).

Sirius Rising. 19 July. Pagan festival coinciding with ancient Egyptian New Year.

Sithny. 4 August. Cornish Celtic saint who holds the distinction of being the patron saint of mad dogs.

Slaying of Isis. See under Samhain.

Slebine. 2 March. Irish saint who was an abbot of Iona. Also called Sleibhin.

Sleibhin. See under Slebine.

Small Litany. See under Litania Minor.

Smoke Sunday. See under Reek Sunday.

Sol Indigis. 9 August. Roman festival of the Living Sun God.

Sol Invictus. 1 January. Ancient 'festival of the unconquerable sun' which developed into the modern Christmas festivities. It dates back as a celebration to at least 218 when the festival and cult of the sun was encouraged by Emperor Elagabalus. It was re-established by Aurelian who built a temple to Sol the sun god in the late 3rd century on 25 December. The day was then celebrated as *Natalis Solis Invicti* or the anniversary of the unconquered sun.

Sol Novus. The festival of the new sun was the same as Sol Invictus (see above).

Solemn Assembly. Jewish celebration.

Solstices. The longest and shortest days of the year. See under Summer Solstice and Winter Solstice.

Sothis-Sirius. 23 July. Pagan.

Spark Sunday. See under Firebrand Sunday.

Spring Equinox. 21 March (Roman 25 March). Equal length days and nights, dates variable depending on location. Also known as the Rites of Spring.

Stephen Protomartyr. 26 December. The Feast of St Stephen was when *King Wenceslaus looked out* in the traditional Christmas carol. In many places sword dancing took place similar to the ceremonies of Plough Monday (see under that entry) when dancers would dance with swords, eventually finishing in the formation of a hexagram made from the intertwined swords. The dances appear to have Viking origins as they were or are performed mostly in areas settled by the Scandinavians during the Viking period. The *Gentleman's Magazine* of 1811 carries a description of the performance of the dances. Unlike the Plough Monday festivities, the St Stephen dances lasted more than one day, finally ending on New Year's Eve. Historically Stephen is believed to have been stoned to death outside the Damascus gate in Jerusalem. In earlier times in Britain, wrens were stoned to death on 26 December in memory of him (see also Wren Day).

Stercus Delatum. 16 June. The last day of the Roman Vestalia festival when all of the rubbish accumulated during the festival was cleared.

Stigmata of Francis of Assisi. 17 September. The (second) feast day of St Francis of Assisi, patron saint of merchants and of Italy is celebrated on 4 October (see also Francis (of Assisi) entry).

Stir Up Sunday. The fifth Sunday before Christmas. So called from the collect in the Book of Common Prayer which reads '*Stir up we beseech thee...*', but taken by congregations as a reminder to stir up the ingredients ready for baking the Christmas cake.

Succot(h). Jewish feast of Tabernacles. A harvest festival which also celebrates all food, friendship, joy and celebration on its final day named Simchat Torah.

Sullani. 26 October to 1 November.

Summer Solstice. 21 June or 11 June in the Old Style calender but variable depending on location. Longest day of the year.

Sunday next before Advent. Twenty-fourth Sunday after Pentecost.

Suovetaurrilia. Roman feast when pigs were sacrificed and eaten.

Suthun. See below under Swithin.

Swithin/Swithun. 2 July. He was Bishop of Winchester from 852 to 862. Also called Suthun. He was born of noble parentage around 805 and was ordained by Helmstan, Bishop of Winchester. He acted as tutor to the children of King Egbert, but was said to be extremely humble, never riding but always travelling on foot. He died 2 July 862 and was buried by his own request outside the north wall of Winchester Cathedral.

Swithin, Translation of. 15 July. Legend states that during his translation (removal of his bones for re-burial) on 15 July 971 to a shrine at the east end of Winchester Cathedral, it began to rain heavily, and did so for 40 days and 40 nights, reflecting the saint's own prediction that he would be buried in heavy rain. The shrine was destroyed in 1538. A weather tradition states that:

Saint Swithin's Day if it should rain, for 40 days so shall remain
But if that day be fine and fair, for 40 days 'twill rain nay maire.

Sylvester. 31 December. Sylvester was Bishop of Rome during the greater part of the reign of Constantine, who allowed him to build many Christian churches in the city. Sylvester is represented in religious art standing on a dragon (symbol of Paganism). He died in 335.

Syprian of Antioch, Martyrdom. 26 September.

T

Tabernacles, Feast of. Jewish festival known also as Succoth.

Tagheam/Taghairm. Moveable Celtic festival, celebrated widely in Scotland and the Isles, often on May Day. In ancient times, involved animal sacrifice and divination.

Tammuz. Jewish fast.

Tan/Tain/Tane/Tin. Variously spelled, the festival of Sant Tan (Holy Fire) was widely celebrated throughout the ancient world, including Britain, by the lighting of fires and beacons on hills and of fires in temples (as at Tempull-na-Teinead, Inismurray, Ireland). Sant Tan was Christianised to St Ann and also possibly St Antony.

Tanabata. 7 July (evening). Celebrated by the Japanese community in Britain. In earlier times it was linked to the lunar calendar and in some places in Japan, the date of celebration is still linked. It is a time of great festivities with lanterns, fireworks and general merriment.

Tang(u)y. 27 November. Male Celtic saint.

Tarquin, Expulsion of. See under Regifugium.

Taurus. 14 May. Roman festival dedicated to Taurus involving bullfighting.

Tebet. Jewish fast.

Teilo. 9 February. Welsh saint. Also known as Deilo.

Telemachus. 1 January. Eastern monk who died circa 351 in the Roman arena when he tried to stop the entertainment because it was a Christian feast day. He was also known as Almacius.

Tenebrae. The last three days of Holy Week when the Tenebrae (Matins and Lauds) are sung in the Catholic Church. The name means 'darkness' and refers to the practice of extinguishing all but one candle.

Teng Chieh. 1 February. The Chinese New Year Lantern Festival which actually marks an end to the New Year celebrations and heralds in the Spring. Celebrated by Chinese communities with firecrackers and rejoicing.

Teresa of Avila/Avica. 15 October. Died 1582. She is depicted as a Carmelite nun whose heart has been pierced by Christ, or an angel with an arrow. She was traditionally called upon in prayer to invoke grace. Historically she is known to have come from a noble Spanish family and to have had nine brothers and three sisters. When her mother died she was put in a convent by her father and in 1533 she became a Carmelite nun against her father's wishes. On St Bartholomew's Day 1562 she founded her own strict Carmelite monastery at Avila, one which was to spread its influence throughout Spain within 20 years. She died on 4 October 1582 at Alva (not to be confused with Avila) and was buried there. Partially successful attempts to make her joint patron saint of Spain (along with St James) proved unpopular. In Britain she is celebrated mainly by Roman Catholics.

Term Days. Scottish system similar to the Quarter Days (see under that entry) in England. Term days were Candlemas, Whit Sunday, Lammas and Martinmas.

Terminalia. 23 February. Roman festival of the god Terminus.

Terra Mater. 15 April. Roman festival that developed into the 'Festival of the Mother Earth'. See under Mother Earth, also. A summer festival with the same name was held from 1 to 3 June inclusive.

Thomas à Becket (of Canterbury). 29 December. St Thomas, Bishop Martyr, died in 1170. He is depicted usually with a sword in his head accompanied by a cross bearer. It was he who instigated Trinity Sunday as a feast day. He was the son of Gilbert Becket, a Norman merchant who lived in London, and Matilda of Caen. Born at Cheapside, he was educated at Merton Priory, Surrey and took up hawking as a hobby. He became an accountant, a lawyer and then in turn, Deacon and Archdeacon of Canterbury, Chancellor of the Exchequer and Archbishop of Canterbury. His close friendship with Henry II eventually soured and Becket fled to plead his case with the Pope. The Pope ruled in favour of Becket much to the King's displeasure. Four knights later assassinated him in his own church of Canterbury. He was buried in the crypt without any ceremony. His body was translated to a shrine behind the high altar in 1220 which remained a centre of pilgrimage until 1538 when Henry VIII had the tomb robbed and the remains burnt.

Thomas à Becket, Translation of. 7 July (1220).

Thomas à Becket, Return of. 2nd December.

Thomas (Apostle). 21 December. Shown in religious icons as carrying either a lance or a carpenter's ruler. He is the patron saint of carpenters and of architects and geometricians. This is the 'doubting Thomas' who did not believe Christ had been resurrected. He is also known as Didymus, both Thomas and Didymus meaning 'twin'. A legend states that Thomas visited the East to find the three Kings who had attended the birth of Jesus and encouraged them to be baptised as Christians. He also went to India to preach, supporting himself by working as a carpenter, and was martyred and buried at Meliapur. His remains were later translated to Goa.

Thomas (Apostle), Translation of. 3 July.

Thomas Aquinas. 7 March. Thomas was known as the 'Angelic Doctor' and was said to be the most learned of all the saints. Born in Aquino, Italy, he was the cousin of Frederick II and the grand-nephew of Emperor Frederick (Barbarossa). He was sent at an early age to the Benedictine abbey of Monte Cassino but left at twelve to assist his father. Because he hardly spoke, he obtained the nickname 'the dumb Sicilian ox' whilst studying for the Dominican order but in spite of this became Second Professor at the Dominican college in Cologne in 1248. Throughout his life, his catchphrase was *Quid Esset Deus?* (What is God?). He died aged 48 in 1274 at Fessa Nuova Abbey, having been taken there by the Benedictines, after falling sick whilst on his travels.

Thomas the Martyr, Translation of. 10 July. Also listed as 3 July in *A History of Whitby* by George Young 1817 (Vol 1, p.337). He was also called Thomas the Apostle.

Thoth (Fast). 19 September.

Three Heirarchs. 30 January. The Holiday of the Three Heirarchs is a festival of the Eastern Orthodox Church which celebrates the lives of St Basil, St Gregory and St John Chrysostum.

Three Kings' Day. 6 January. See under Epiphany.

Tiarnach. See under Tigernach of Clones.

Tibernalia. 17 August. Roman festival dedicated to Tiberinus.

Tid. Fifth Sunday before Easter Day. The Sundays before Easter were remembered by the rhyme: '*Tid, Mid, Mizeray, Carling, Palm and Easter Day.*' Tid is a Scottish word indicating 'tide', meaning a fit time or condition (eg as in Eastertide).

Tigernach of Clones. 4 April. Irish saint also known as Tiarnach.

Timothy. 24 January. Stoned to death in AD 97 when he tried to break up the Pagan festival of Katagogian. He was the disciple of the Apostle Paul and is the patron saint of those who suffer from stomach troubles. This is said to be because he insisted on taking wine *'for the sake of the health of the stomache'*.

Timothy and Appollinarius. 23 August.

Transfiguration. 6 August. Commemorating the story in the Bible of Christ being transformed in appearance upon a mountain. Celebrated 19 August in the Old Style calendar

Trasimene, Defeat of. 22 June. Roman festival to remember the dead in their defeat at Lake Trasimene.

Translation of... See under saint's name.

Trevor/Treveur. 8 November. Celtic saint of Brittany. Patron saint of Carhaix, Camlez and Kergloff. Feast day celebrated widely elsewhere.

Trial of King Edward. 20 June.

Tridium. Three-day religious festival beginning on the evening of Holy Thursday and ending on the evening of Easter Sunday.

Triduana's Fast. Celtic saint who is said to have plucked out her eyes rather than marry a suitor. Her shrine and well at Restalrig, Scotland was renowned for its power to heal the eyes. A fast of three days was celebrated in her honour. She may be the same as St Modwenna and Medana who all have 'eye stories' attached to them, as does St Lucy.

Trifine. 21 July. Female Celtic saint.

Trinity Sunday. Sunday nearest 29 May. This began generally to be accepted as a festival in the 14th century though it had been instigated in 1170 by Thomas à Becket.

Triumph of the Cross. Originating in September 335 during the dedication of the basilica built on the supposed site of Golgotha. It later became a celebration of the reign of Emperor Constantine and his religious acts. Also known as Holy Cross Day.

Tubilustrium. 23 March. Roman festival 'of the purification of trumpets'.

Tudful. The date of the feast of Tudful the Martyr appears not to be documented, though it seems to have been once widely celebrated, particularly in Wales. This may be the same saint as Tudual (see below).

Tudual. 30 November. Male Celtic saint, possibly the same as Tudful (see above).

Tudy. 9 June. Celtic saint of Brittany. Celebrated elsewhere.

Twelfth Day/Night. 6 January. Epiphany. The evening preceding it was known as Twelfth Night and was celebrated by eating a 'Twelfth Cake' containing a bean or coin. The person getting the piece which contained it was declared King or Queen of the festivities which marked the end of Christmas.

Tysoe. See under Tysylio (below).

Tysylio. Celtic saint, celebrated in the longest place name in Wales: Llanfairpwllgwyngyllgogerychwyrndrobwllllantysiliogogoch. Probably the same as St Tysoe (also Welsh).

U

Unconquerable Sun Festival. See under Sol Invictus.

Universal King. See under Stir Up Sunday.

Uny. Feast day unknown. Once associated with Redruth in Cornwall but evidently overtaken by St Ruth as patron of the town according to once popular folklore.

Upp Helly Aa. 30 January. A Pagan version of Septuagesima when tar barrels were burnt and, as at Lerwick in the Shetlands, a torchlight procession was organised, culminating in the burning of a boat.

Ursula (Virgin Martyr). 21 October. Many authorities consider Ursula only a legend. She is depicted as a princess holding an arrow or an axe in her hand. She is the patron saint of teachers, youths, schoolgirls, drapers and maidens. In legend she was the daughter of the king of Cornwall who prior to an arranged marriage set sail for the Rhine on a three year voyage with 11,000 handmaidens in eleven galleys. All were slain by the Huns using axes. Whitesands College was dedicated to her, as

Upp Helly Aa – A 1930s picture of the Viking boat ceremony at Lerwick in Scotland.

was the English church of St Mary Axe, its full dedication name being *St Mary the Virgin, Ursula and the Eleven Thousand Virgins*. One of the church's former artefacts was an axe head, said to have been brought back from the site on the Rhine where the virgins had been executed in 451.

V

Valentine. 14 February. See also Lupercalia from which it evolved. Legend tells us that St Valentine was a priest who secretly married couples against the dictum of Emperor Claudius of Rome who had ruled that Roman soldiers were not allowed to marry as it made them bad warriors. Valentine was imprisoned when caught and was beheaded on 14 February 271 (or 270?). Other martyrs named Valentine are also involved in various stories of the origins of Valentine's Day.

Vedast. 1 October.

Vedast and Amanus. 6 February.

Vediovis. 1 January, also 7 March. Roman festival.

Veiovis. 21 May. Roman festival.

Venerable Bede. 27 May.

Veneralia. 1 April. Roman festival dedicated to Venus Verticordia and Fortuna Virilis.

Venus. 23 April, also 23 and 24 June and 19 July. Roman festivals.

Venus, Festival of. 10 March, later changing to 19 March.

Venus Verticordia. See under Veneralia.

Vernal Equinox. 21 March (Roman 25 March). Equal length days and nights – dates variable depending on location. The Spring Equinox. See also Ostara.

Veronica. 13 January. Veronica was from Milan and was known in her lifetime as Veronica de Binasco.

Veronica (Bernice). 4 February. Said to be an ordinary woman who lived on the road to Calvary. Christ, carrying his cross, fell at her door and she wiped his face with a napkin. The napkin was eventually found to have Christ's face imprinted upon it. The 'Veronica' became a sacred artifact, being likened to and sometimes confused with the famous Turin Shroud.

Vertumnalia. 13 August. Roman festival dedicated to Vertumnus.

Vesta. 13 February, 28 April and 1 March. Single-day Roman festivals of light when Vestal Virgins led candle-lit processions. These occurred at other times and were often one-day features within a longer festival period.

Vestalia. 7 to 15 June. The Roman festival of the Vestal Virgins who kept a constant flame burning at the temple of Vesta, goddess of the hearth and home. Vesta was the sister of Zeus. 7 June was a particular holiday for fishermen.

Vica Pota. 5 January. The last day of Compitalia when in Roman times the shrine of Vica Pota was rededicated and blessed.

Victoria Day. Third Monday in May (Scotland).

Vigil of St Mark. See under Mark's Vigil.

Vinalia Prioria. 23 April. Roman festival dedicated to Venus.

Vinalia Rustica. 19 August. A country festival originally dedicated to the grape harvest. It dates back long before Roman times and was still in existence in the 18th century.

Vincent de Paul. 27 September. A former shepherd from a comparatively wealthy farming family near Bayonne, he went on to become a lay preacher and then to form the first order of unenclosed Sisters of Mercy, assisting him to take care of the poor. He also provided centres for lay preachers, caring for animals, the poor, orphaned children and any creature needing assistance. He is patron of all charitable works. Vincent de Paul died a natural death on 27 September 1660.

Vincent the Martyr. 22 January. Patron saint of winegrowers, he suffered from a major speech impediment. A native of Saragossa in Spain, he was educated by the local bishop, Valerius and was ordained as a deacon. During the Christian persecutions, Valerius was exiled but Vincent was captured and tortured to death. His body was thrown into the sea, but was recovered and buried in the main church of Valencia.

Vine Festival. 21 September.

Virgin Mary, Annunciation. 25 March.

Virgin Mary, Assumption. 15 August or 28 August in Old Style calendar.

Virgin Mary, Immaculate Conception. 8 December.

Virgin Mary, Immaculate Heart. 22 August.

Virgin Mary, Nativity. 8 September or 21 September in the Old Style calendar. The feast is said to have been initiated by Pope Servius in 695 after a monk had a vision of angels who told him they were singing to celebrate the Virgin Mary's day of birth. A chapel at Ephesus, Turkey is said to have been built upon the site of the house in which she served the last of her days. It

*Virgin Mary (Immaculate Conception) –
A Victorian engraving illustrating the
Immaculate Conception, celebrated on 8
December.*

serves as a shrine to this day. She died in Ephesus on 15 August in an unknown year. See also under Holy Name, Mary Magdalene and Our Lady.

Virgin Mary, Purification of. 2 February. See also Lupercalia from which it is said to have evolved.

Virgin Mary, Rosary of. First Sunday in October but variable. Celebrated also as Our Lady of the Rosary.

Virgin Mary, Queenship of. 31 May. Equates to Mothers Day

Virgin Mary, Sorrow of. Date variable since the 13th century. Now no longer celebrated.

Virgin Mary, Visitation. 2 July. Celebrates the visitation of Mary to her cousin Elizabeth.

Vitus. 15 June. Christianised holy day that developed from the Pagan 'Rising Nile Day'. He is the patron saint of dancers, actors, comedians and of course those suffering from St Vitus' Dance. The feast day is unusual in that it also honoured Crescentia (nurse of St Vitus who suffered from epilepsy) and her husband Modestus who was his tutor.

Vocem Juncunditatis. The Latin name for Rogation. See under that entry.

Volturnalia. 27 August. Roman festival dedicated to Volturnus.

Vulcan. 23 May. Single-day Roman festival dedicated to Vulcan.

Vulcanalia. 22 August.

W

Wakes. Moveable feasts, also called Love Feasts. These had no connection with the wakes held at funerals or with the gatherings known as love feasts organised by Wesley during the early days of Methodism. An early explanation of wakes, quoting a Dr Kennet as the source, is discussed in the *Spectator* (no. 161-September 4th, 1711): '*These wakes, says he, were in imitation of the ancient αγαπω or Love-Feasts; and were first established in England by Pope Gregory the Great, who in an epistle to Melitus the Abbot gave order that they should be kept in sheds or arbories made up with branches and boughs of trees round the church. He adds that this laudable custom of wakes prevailed for many ages, till the nice Puritans began to exclaim against it as a remnant of Popery; and by degrees the precise humour grew so popular, that at an Exeter assizes the Lord Chief Baron Walter made an order for the suppression of all wakes; but on Bishop Laud's complaining of this innovating humour, the King commanded the order be reversed.*' Whether or not these original love feasts or wakes were a left-over from the earlier 'amatory masses' instigated by the church during the days of the plague is uncertain. These amatory masses are said to have involved church services in which the priest in charge would have permission to have ritual sexual intercourse with female parishioners in an effort to increase the greatly depleted population of the country.

Walburga/Walpurga. Eve of May Day/1 May (Roman) and 25 February (monastic calendar). St Walburga, 710-776/7, was born in Devon. She was abbess of Heidenheim and is said to be the patron saint of all who seek protection from magic arts. Her name is also spelt Walpurde and Walpurgis. The eve of May Day came to be called Walpurgis Night.

Walpurde. See Walburga, above.

Walpurgis. See Walburga, above.

Waltheof. Abbot of Melrose and ward or stepson of David I of Scotland.

Wayzgoose. Moveable holiday for people employed in the printing trade and sometimes other trades. It varied from a full week's holiday to an annual day-trip.

Week of Forgiveness. Early name for Holy Week.

Week of the Holy Passion. Holy Week.

Weeks, Feast of. Jewish festival of Pentecost.

Well Dressing Day. 26 May but varies with location. See also under Ascension.

Wenceslaus. 28 September. Patron saint of Czechoslovakia but associated with Christmas festivities throughout Europe.

Werburga. Date uncertain. His restored shrine survives at Chester Abbey.

Wesak. Festival to celebrate the birth, enlightenment and death of the Buddha (Siddhartha). It is traditional for Buddhists to decorate their homes or places of worship with flowers, streamers and flags on this day and to wash and clean Buddhist shrines.

Whit. See under Whitsuntide.

Whit Monday. Day following Whit Sunday and a traditional English holiday.

Whit Sunday. Originally the Sunday nearest 26 May, then 15 May. Also called Pentecost. The term comes from 'white' indicating the white robes worn by those newly baptised on Whit Sunday. In Old English it was known as Hwita Sunnandaeg (White Sunday).

White Sunday. See under Whit Sunday.

Whitsuntide. Known colloquially as Whit or Whit Week. The week following Whit Sunday.

Wilfrid. 12 October. Born in Northumbria in 634, Wilfred was educated at Lindisfarne. He travelled to Canterbury and Rome and was one of the chief spokesmen for adopting the Roman religious rule at the Synod of Whitby in 664. He was appointed Bishop of York but whilst in France, where he was to be consecrated, (St) Chad was appointed in his place. Wilfred began many monasteries such as at Ripon, Oundle, Stamford and Hexham during his lifetime and was also Bishop in Mercia, eventually serving in York and in Lichfield. At one stage he was accused of forging a Papal Bull and was imprisoned for it. He retired to the north, spending his time at Hexham and Ripon where he was buried after dying on a journey to Oundle Abbey in 709. It has been said of Wilfred that he had an equal capacity for making genuine friends and genuine enemies.

Wilfrid, Translation of. 24 April.

William. A native of Perth, Scotland, who was murdered near Rochester whilst on his way to the Holy Land. His shrine in Rochester drew Benedictine pilgrims whose offerings were used to rebuild the cathedral choir.

Winifred. 3 November.

Winnin(g)/Wynnin(g). 21 January. Celtic.

Winter Solstice. 21 December. Variable depending on location – shortest day of the year.

Witches' Night. 17th century name for Midsummer's Eve when witches were said to gather to renew their vows.

Witchwood Day. 2 May. Also known as St Helen's Day. It was traditional on this day to collect branches from rowan trees, referred to as Witch Wood or Wiccan Wood. This was taken indoors where it would be left until it rotted the following year in order to protect homes from witches. Pieces of rowan were also made into objects and carried in the pockets or purses of villagers as good luck talismen.

Whirling Sunday. Scottish version of Carling Sunday.

Woden and Berchta. 25 December to 6 January. This was the period when the god Woden and his wife Berchta decended from the realm of the gods and lived an earthly existence.

Wol(och). 29 January, with a fair on 30 January. Scottish saint also called St Mac Woloch. May be the same as Wolvela. See under Gudwell.

Wolvela. See under Wol(och) and Gudwell.

Wren Day. Varied in December but generally 24/25 or 26. Wren Day survived in the Isle of Man until the 1900s but was once a European-wide occurrence. On the appointed day a wren (considered King of the Birds) was ritually killed (generally stoned to death) and was buried in a sombre funeral service. The ancient rhyme *Who killed cock robin* refers to killing the robin (or 'spidogge', as it was once known) in mistake for the wren. This came about because any small bird was referred to as a spidogge in some areas. The wren in mythology was the 'stealer of the fire' and in northern France they believed that a golden wren was credited with the power to make fire by stealing it from heaven (similar to the Greek myth of Prometheus). See also Stephen Protomartyr.

Wroth Silver Day. 11 November. Day when the annual payments of tenants were collected by an officer of the Duke of Buccleuch at Knightlow Hill in Warwickshire.

Wulfstan. 19 January. Born in 1009, Wulfstan was the last of the Anglo-Saxon saints and a former bishop of Worcester. His parents who were of lowly stock retired to a monastery in their old age, possibly encouraging him to take up the habit of a monk. Following the Norman Conquest, he was belittled for not speaking French and was looked down on by the new authorities. He was a great opponent of slave trading and preached often at Bristol docks. He died 19 January 1095.

X

Xmas. Though now considered a commercial form of the word Christmas, the term was used anciently because the cross (X) was considered an acceptable symbol to indicate the word Christ.

Y

Yom Kippur. Jewish Day of Atonement.

Yule (begins). 21 December (eve of). See also under Jul.

Yule Day. 25 December.

Z

Zetesis. 28 October.

Zita. 27 April. Died 1278. She is the patron saint of all domestic servants and is depicted as a servant maid who carries a rosary and a key.

APPENDIX I

CALENDAR OF SAINTS DAYS, FEAST DAYS, FASTS AND FESTIVALS

JANUARY

1 Aesculapius; Almacius; Circumcision; Compitalia; Fainche of Rossory; Gamelia Festival; Juno; New Year's Day; Odilo; Oissine; Sol Invictus; Vediovis
2 Isadore; Macarius
3 Genevieve; Levenez
4 Benedict (Bishop); Fianait
5 Ciar of Kilkeary; Edward the Confessor; Simon Stylites; Vica Pota
6 Christmas (old); Epiphany; Melan; Meryn Muaddnat of Drumcliffe; Three Kings' Day; Twelfth Day
7 Cedd(e); Rock Day
8 Justicia; Lucian
9 Adrian; Aganolia; Agonalia; Edana; Faolan; Jose, Translation of
10
11 Carmentalia; Juturnalia
12 Compitalia of Lares
13 Hilary; Remigius; Veronica
14 Felix; Festival of the Ass; Kentigern(a); Mungo
15 Ide
16 Concordia
17 Anthony/Antony; Felicitas
18 Prisca (Virgin and Martyr)
19 Brevelaer (Bishop); Canute; Fornacalia; Knut's Day; Wulfstan
20 Fabian and Sebastian; Fabian (Bishop and Martyr); Sebastian (Martyr)
21 Agnes (Virgin and Martyr); Winnin(g)
22 Lonan Finn; Vincent (Martyr)
23 Emerentiana; Ildephonsus
24 Cadoc; Katagogian; Pagnalia; Sementivae; Timothy
25 Ananius of Damascus; Burns Night; Dwyn; Paul, Conversion of
26 Conan of Man; Polycarp
27 Devote; John Chrysostom; Julian
28 Agnes, Nativity of; Eochaid (Bishop of Tallaght)
29 Francis of Sales; Gidas; Wol(och)

30 Altar of Peace, Dedication of; King Charles I; King Charles the Martyr; Three Heirarchs; Upp Helly Aa
31 Aed; Aodhan of Fern; Maughold

FEBRUARY

1 Berched; Breched; Brede; Bride; Brigantia; Brighid; Brigit; Candlemas; Fast of February; Festival of Lights; Festival of the Earth Mother; Ffraid; Ignatius; Imbolc; Juno Sopista; Laa'l Breeshey; Light Festival; Oilmelc
2 Christ's Presentation in the Temple; Meallan/Maelrhub(ha); Virgin Mary, Purification of
3 Anskar; Blaise; Caelfind
4 Gilbert of Sempringham; Veronica (Bernice)
5 Agatha (Virgin and Martyr); Augustus; Concordia; Pater Patria
6 Brandubh; Dorothy (Virgin and Martyr); Macha of Killiney; Vedas and Amanus
7 Derrien; Romuald; Ronan/Ronain
8 Lassa(air) of Meath
9 Branwalather; Caireach; Ronan of Lismore; Teilo
10 Paul, Shipwreck of; Scholastica
11 Gobnait
12 Benedict Biscop; Callisto; Olaille; Riok
13 Edward King and Martyr (first translation); Fallen Fabii; Faunalia; Faunus; Hermenilda; Parantalia; Vesta
14 Conran; Conval; Valentine
15 Berarch; Lupercalia
16 Juliana (Martyr)
17 Finnsech of County Meath; Fornax; Gireg; Quirinalia
18 Aedammair; Colman
19
20
21 Feralia
22 Caristia; Peter, Chair of
23 Juliana; Milburga; Terminalia
24 Matthias; Regifugium; Roparzh
25 Koulma; Walburga
26
27 Equiria; Horonina; Odran; Onran
28 Ernine; Oswald (Bishop)
29

MARCH

1 Aubyn; David (Archbishop); Feriae Marti; Matronalia; Vesta
2 Chad; Nonna; Slebine
3 Comgan; Gwenole
4 Adrian (Martyr); Casimir
5 Comgan; Piran
6 Brandubh; Gwennec
7 Felicity and Perpetua; Perpetua (Martyr); Thomas Aquinas; Vediovis
8 Senan of Iniscathy
9 Costentyn; Francis of Rome; Melle
10 Kanna; Kavan; Venus, Festival of
11 Angus; Aonghus; Oengus Ceile De
12 Gregory the Great; Hugh of Avalon; Pol
13
14 Equiria; Mamuralia
15 Anna Perenna; Ides of March (Assassination of Julius Caesar); Jupiter
16 Abban mac us Cormaich; Bacchanalia; Eugenia
17 Gertrude; Joseph of Arimathea; Patrick (Bishop and Saint)
18 Cyril; Edward (King and Martyr)
19 Festival of Venus; Joseph (Father of Christ); Quinquatrus; Venus, Festival of
20 Cuthbert (Bishop)
21 Benedict, Abbot (Benedictines); Spring Equinox; Vernal Equinox
22 Cybele and Attis
23 Tubilustrium
24 Fast of March; Gabriel (Archangel); March Fast; Rex Comitiavit
25 Alban Eiler (Light of the Earth); Annunciation; Bird Day; Dismas; Eostra; Eostra's Day; Festival of Joy; Hillaria (Roman Festival); Lady Day; Spring/Vernal Equinox (Roman); Virgin Mary, Annunciation
26
27
28 Christopher, Martyrdom of
29 Gladez
30 Salus
31 Luna, Festival of; Moon Festival

APRIL

1 April Fools Day; Ceres; Gilbert of Caithness; Holy Fools Day; Huntigowok Day; Veneralia
2 Francis (of Paola); Mary of Egypt; Pleiades
3 Richard (Bishop)
4 Ambrose; Cybele and Attis (Roman); Festival of the Great Mother; Isidore; Magalesia; Tigernach of Clones
5 Fortuna
6 Bearchan
7 Annunciation (Old Style); Goron
8
9 Lumeria
10 Megalesia
11 Guthlac; Leo the Great
12
13 Egg Day
14 Isis; Ithon
15 Fordicidia; Mother Earth Festival; Ruadan; Terra Mater
16 Donan; Magnus of Orkney.
17 Donnan; Eochaid
18
19 Alphege; Cerealia
20
21 Anselm (Bishop); Palilia
22 Ceallachan
23 Eoghan; George; Horus (Slaying of Set); Ibor; Venus; Vinalia Prioria
24 Mark's Vigil; Melitus; Wilfred, Translation of
25 Mark (Evangelist); Robigalia
26 Edward (King and Martyr), Translation of
27 Anastasius; Floria/Floralia; Maughold; Newlyn(a); Zita
28 Vesta
29 Catherine of Siena; Endelyon
30 Erkenwald; May Eve

MAY

1 Amalthea; Bealtine (Beltain); Beltane; Breoc; Briec/Brieg; Cetsamhain; Corentyn; Dippy Day/Dipping Day; Festival of Fools (Roman); Festival of the Flowers; Floral Day; Fools Holy Day; Furry Day (Floral Day); Gesling Day; Gluvias; Goodfire

Day; Gosling Day; Horse Ribbon Day; Jack in the Green Parade; James the Less(er); Lares Praestites; May Day; Oissine; Philip; Philip and James; Rood Day; Roodmas

2 Athanasius; Helen; Setsamhain; Tagheam/Taghairm; Walburga; Witchwood Day

3 Achilles; Alexander; Bona Dea; Cairbre (Bishop); Carbry; Chiron; Conlaed; Cross, Invention of; Eventius; Ewen; Glewas; Hercules; Rood Day

4 Monica

5 Festival of Flags; Flags, Feast of

6 John Before the Latin Gate; John the Evangelist (The Divine); Serapis Mysteries; Serf/Serif/Serv

7 Benedict (Pope); John of Beverley; Lemuria; Letardus; Rood Day

8 Floral Day; Furry Day; Mens; Michael, Apparition of; Michael's Day; Odran

9 Lemura (Expulsion of Ghosts); Liberation Day; Nicholas, Translation of

10 Comhgahall; Cowel; Gordianus and Epimachus; Orion

11 Expulsion of Ghosts; Matuta

12 Ludi Martiales; Mars Ultor; Nereus and Achilleus; Pancras

13 Quinquatrus

14 Gil of Santiem; Taurus

15 Dympna; Ludi Mercery; Mercury (Mercuralia)

16 Bre(a)nden / Breannain / Brendon; Carantoc; Honoratus of Amiens

17 Dea Dia; Madron

18 Eric

19 Dominic, Translation of; Dorothy (Virgin and Martyr); Dunstan (Bishop); Erwan

20 Bernardine; Bernadino of Siena; Castor and Pollux

21 Colan; Collen; Helena; Janus; Veiovis

22 Luisech

23 Crimthann; Vulcan

24 Dabhaid; David; Rex Comitavit

25 Aldhelm; Francis, Translation of

26 Augustine (Archbishop); Be(a)can Day; Diana (Roman); Prosperine; Well Dressing Day

27 Bede (The Venerable)

28 Augustine (Archbishop); Lanfranc; Removal Terms

29 Ambarvalia; Bona; King Charles II; Oak Apple Day

30 Joan (of Arc)
31 Angela Merici; Queenship of Virgin Mary

JUNE

1 Carna; Juno; Nicomede (Martyr); Pilgrimage to Purgatory; Ronan/Ronain; Terra Mater
2 Erasmus; Marcellinus and Peter; Odo
3 Bellona; Caemgen; Caohimin; Kevin
4 Beryan; Breaca; Hercules the Guardian; Peadar; Pedrog
5 Boniface
6 Claude of Besancon; Jarlath; Neven
7 Meriadec; Meryasec; Vestalia
8 Alphege; Medard and Gildard
9 Calum; Colm Cille; Columba (Abbot); Crassus, Defeat of; Edmund, Translation of; Tudy
10 Baithene; Mairead
11 Barnabas; Concord; Fortuna; Matralia; Summer Solstice (Old Calendar)
12 Meven
13 Aesculapius; Antony of Padua; Cairell of Tir Ros; Damhnait; Paul (Apostle); Quinquatrus Minusculoe
14 Basil; Simon (Archbishop)
15 Eadburga; Nile Day; Rising Nile Day; Vitus
16 Ciricus and Julitta; Stercus Dalatum
17 Alban; Botulph/Botuloph; Herve; Ludi Piscatori; Neython
18 Mark and Marcellianus
19 Gervais and Prothasius
20 Edward (King and Martyr), Second Translation of; Edward (King and Martyr), Trial of; Hippolytus (Roman)
21 Alban Hefin; Alban Heruin; Janus; Litha; Midsummer's Day; Oak Festival; Oraea; Summer Solstice
22 Alban; Trasimene (Defeat)
23 Etheldreda; Fast of June; Hans; John's Eve; June Fast; Midsummer Bonfire Day; Venus
24 Bannockburn Day; Bartholomew of Farne; Fata; Fors Fortuna; John the Baptist, Nativity of
25 Eligius; Fillan; Moluag/Moluoc
26 John and Paul
27 Aestes; Our Lady of Perpetual Help
28 Austell; Fast of June; June Fast; Leo
29 Beatrice; Peter (Apostle); Peter and Paul

30 Batilda; Paul, Commemoration of

JULY

1 Ceres
2 Swithin/Swithun; Virgin Mary, Visitation of
3 Garmon; Killian; Thomas (Apostle), Translation of
4 Martin, Translation of; Pax
5 Irenus; Ludi Appolinaris; Morwenna; Poplifugia
6 Apollo; Moninne of Killevy; Nolwen
7 Hedda; Nonae Caprotinae; Thomas à Becket; Tanabata
8 Grimbald; Margaret (Queen)
9 Garbhan
10 Thomas the Martyr, Translation of
11 Benedict (Abbot), Translation of
12 Orangeman's Day
13 Mildred; Neot
14
15 Swithin, Translation of
16 Helier; Mac Darra of Connemara; Osmund, Translation of; Our Lady of Mount Carmel
17 Kenelm
18 Arnulf
19 Lucaria; Sirius Rising; Venus
20 Margaret (of Antioch)
21 Trifine
22 Mary Magdalene
23 Apollinaris the Martyr and Timothy; Neptunalia; Seva; Sothis; Sirius
24 Christina; Declan; Fast of July (July Fast)
25 Christopher; Furrinalia; Iago; James the Apostle (The Greater)
26 Anne
27
28
29 Felix and Faunstinus; Martha; Olaf; Silyen
30 Abdon and Sennes
31 German/Germaine/Germanus; Ignatius; Ignatius Loyola

AUGUST

1 Bread Festival; Festival of the Grain (Grain Festival); Gule of August; Harvest Festival; Lammas; Lughnassa(dh); Peter ad Vincula

2 Our Lady of the Angels

3

4 Dominic; Gamaliel; Nicodemus; Sithny

5 Oswald (King); Our Lady of the Snow; Rush Bearing Day

6 Felicissimus and Agapitus; Transfiguration

7 Donat; Jesus, Name of; Osyth

8 Ciriacus; Colman (Ireland)

9 Feidhlimidh; Sol Indigis

10 Lawrence (Martyr); Ops

11

12 Clare (Abbess); Festival of Lights; Hercules (Roman); Janbryght

13 Diana; Hippolytus; Hypolit; Nemoralia; Vertumnalia

14 Eusebius

15 Virgin Mary, Assumption

16 Arzhel

17 Portunalia, Tibernalia

18 Helena

19 Magnus; Transfiguration (Old Style); Vinalia Rustica

20 Bernard (of Clairvaux)

21 Consualia; Ludi Consualia

22 Immaculate Heart of Mary (Virgin); Vulcanalia

23 August Fast (Fast of August); Juturna; Nemesia; Timothy and Appollinarius

24 Bartholomew; Ceres; Owen

25 Hilda, Festival of; Genesius; Louis; Maree; Mouree; Opec(on-siva)/Opiconsivia

26 Augustine (Archbishop); Bergwin; Edem

27 Volturnalia

28 Augustinus Magnus; Augustine of Hippo; Hermes; Virgin Mary, Assumption (Old Style)

29 John the Baptist, Beheading of

30 Felix and Audactus; Rewen

31 Aidan; Cuthbeg; Eanswith

SEPTEMBER

1 Egidius; Giles/Gillies; Priscus

2 Antonius

3 Gregory the Great, Ordination of; Marinus

4 Cuthbert, Translation of; Ludi Magni

5 Bertin; Ludi Romani

6

 7 Dunstan, Translation of; Elizabeth II (Queen), Official Birthday; Enurchus (Bishop); Eunerches
 8 Adrian (Hadrian) the Martyr; Horn(ing) Day; Virgin Mary, Nativity of
 9 Cera; Ciaran; Horn Dance Day
10
11 Deiniol; Glen
12 Ailbe; Holy Name of Mary
13 Augustine, Translation of
14 Cornelius and Cyprian; Cyprian; Exaltation of the Holy Cross; Holy Cross Day
15 Battle of Britain Day; Mirren; Romani
16 Cornelius (Pope); Edith; Euphemia; Lucian and Geminian; Ninian
17 Lambert; Francis of Assisi, Stigmata of
18 Joseph of Cupertino
19 Fast of Thoth; Januarius
20 Fast of September (September Fast)
21 Alban Elfred; Alban Elued; Autumn Equinox; Festival of the Vine; Mabon; Mabyn; Matthew (Evangelist); Michael (Micul) of the Isles; Midautumn Day; Vine Festival; Virgin Mary, Nativity of (Old Style)
22 Maurice (and others)
23 Adamnan/Adomnan; Ceres; Elevation of the Life Giving Cross; Elusinia; Neptune
24 Robert of Knaresborough
25 Ceolfrith(i); Donan; Fin(n)barr; Firminus
26 Cyprian and Justina; Justina, Martyrdom of; Mawgan; Syprian of Antioch, Martyrdom of
27 Barr(i); Cosmas and Damian; Elevation of the Life Giving Cross (Old Style); Vincent de Paul
28 Bernard of Feltres; Konan; Mac Dara of Connemara; Wenceslaus
29 Archangel(s), Festival of; Michael and All Angels; Michael (Archangel)
30 Heironymus; Honorius; Jerome (Cardinal); Leri

OCTOBER

 1 Ceres; Fides; Melorius; Remigius; Vedast
 2 Leger
 3 Klervi

 4 Francis (of Assisi); Francis of Assisi, Stigmata of

 5

 6 Arzhur; Bruno; Faith; Hugh, Translation of; Nigasius

 7 Marcellus and Apuleius; Osith

 8 Morgan(a/e)

 9 Cadwaladr/Cadwaller; Denis/Denys; Felicitas

10 Francis (Borgia); Gereon; Paulinus

11 Augustinus Magnus, Translation of; Cainnech; Callneach; Coinneach; Lomman; Meditrinalia

12 Edwin; Fortuna Redux; Wilfrid

13 Cowan; Edward the Confessor, Translation of; Finnsech of
County Tyrone; Fontinalia; Gilbert, Translation of; Lucia

14 Calixtus; Enora; Gobban of Killamery; Manacca; Seleven

15 Donatian; Equiria; Teresa of Avila/Avica

16 Ciar of Kilkeary; Lord Mayor's Day; Michael in Monte Tumba

17 Etheldreda, Translation of

18 Daigh of Inishkeen; Gwen Teirbron; Luke (Evangelist)

19 Armilustrium; Frideswide (Abbess); Meallan/Maelrub(ha)

20

21 Dunstan, Ordination of; Marcan of Clonenagh; Ursula (Virgin
Martyr)

22 Mary Salome

23

24 Maglore; Raphael (Archangel)

25 Alor; Crispin(ian); Henry V Day; John of Beverley, Translation
of

26 Demetrios; Sullani

27 Fast of October (October Fast)

28 Festival of Zetesis; Jude (Apostle); Simon Zelotes; Simon and
Jude; Zetesis

29 Lord Mayor's Day

30 Beth(og)

31 Erc(us)/Erghe/Erth; Fast of October (October Fast); Hallowe'en

NOVEMBER

 1 All Saints Day; Cadfan; Cairbre; Dead, Festival of; Samhain;
Shone/Shonee/Shony Day

 2 All Souls' Day; Camps, Feast of; Caohime; Eustace; Festival of
Camps

 3 Gwen(frewi); Hugh of Liege; Malarchy of Armagh; Winifred

 4 Cleer; Plebian Games; Plebii

5 Bonfire Night (Guy Fawkes Night); Papist Conspiracy
6 Leonard; Milyan
7 Efflam
8 Trevor/Treveur
9 Lord Mayor's Day
10 Just
11 Armistice Day (Remembrance Day); Beggars Day; Blane; Martin; Martinmas; Menna
12 Gulval; Kristen; Livinus; Machonna
13 Brice; Columba; Epulum Jovis; Juno; Jupiter
14 Erkenwald, Translation of; Laurence (O'Toole); Lorcan O'Tuathail
15 Cywair; Feronia; Gower; Lea; Malo; Mawe
16 Aeluric; Alphege, Ordination of; Edmund (Archbishop); Govren
17 Anianus; Bees; Hilda, Death of; Hugh of Avalon; Hugh of Lincoln
18 Ceres; Kevern
19 Elizabeth of Hungary
20 Dasius; Edmund (King and Martyr)
21 Our Lady's Presentation at the Temple
22 Aziliz; Catherine (Virgin Martyr); Cecilia
23 Clement (of Rome); Felicity
24 Columbanus; Chrysogonus
25 Catherine (Virgin Martyr); Katherine
26 Linus
27 Alan; Tang(u)y
28 Heodez; Removal Term (Scotland)
29 Fast of November (November Fast); Fianait
30 Andrew; Creed; Tudual

DECEMBER

1 Alar; Faunalia; Poseidon
2 Francis Xavier; Thomas à Becket, Return of
3 Birin/Birinus; Bona Dea; Ceres
4 Athene's Day; Barbara; Osmund
5 Faunus
6 Nicholas (Bishop of Myra)
7 Ambrose (Bishop), Father of the Latins; Azenor
8 Buthek; Immaculate Conception (of Virgin Mary)
9 Opalia
10

11 Agonalia; Agonia/Agonium; Damasus; Deniol/Denoel; Janus

12 Kaourantin

13 Ember Day; Jose; Luciadagann; Lucy (Virgin and Martyr); Opalia; Sementivae

14

15 Consualia

16 Judikael; Ninth Day; O Sapienta

17 Saturnalia

18 Godric of Finchale

19 Opalia

20 December Fast

21 Alban Arthuan; Athmael; Arthur, Light of; Geola; Jul/Yul; Midwinter's Day; Rebirth (of the Sun); Thomas (Apostle); Winter Solstice; Yule

22 Briac; Eimhin; Janus

23 Gwenrael; Larenta/Larentalia/Laurentalia; Little Christmas

24 Adam and Eve Day; Christmas Eve; December Fast; Mothers' Night (Night of the Mothers); Wren Day

25 Christmas Day; Dionysus; Helios; Horus; Mithras/Mitra/Mitras; Opiconsivia; Woden and Berchta; Yule Day

26 Antony (Cornish); Boxing Day; Morrow of Christmas; Saturn Day; Stephen Protomartyr

27 John the Evangelist (The Divine)

28 Childermas; Cross Day; Holy Innocents

29 Thomas à Becket

30 Egwin

31 Angerona; Burning of the Clavie; Divalia; Hogmanay; Hogunnaa; New Year's Eve; Sylvester

APPENDIX II

DATE-RELATED PHRASES AND TERMS YOU MAY COME ACROSS IN DOCUMENTS AND DEEDS

after Pentecost. All Sundays after Trinity Sunday (Roman Catholic).

after Trinity. All Sundays after Trinity Sunday (Church of England).

ACE. After Common Era. Used as a 'politically correct' form of AD.

AH. Indicative of the Moslem calendar.

AM. Indicative of the Jewish calendar.

Annus Christus (AC). Same as BC.

Anno Domini (AD). Years after the birth of Christ (ie, Year of our Lord).

Ano Lucis (AL). Year of light, based on the biblical book of Genesis I:3 using Ushers's Notation that the creation of the world took place in 4000 BC, ie AL dates vary by 4,000 years from those of AD.

ante. Before.

annuitant. Person receiving a yearly pension often on a set day.

AUC. Indicative of the Roman Calendar (Ab Urbe Condita).

BC. Years Before Christ.

BCE. Before Common Era. Used as a 'politically correct' form of BC.

biennially. Occuring every second year (often confused with biannually).

biannually. Occuring twice in one year (often confused with biennially).

calendae. First day of each month.

calendarum. First day of each month.

canonical hours. There were seven of these in the western church: (1) Nocturns or Matins and Lauds before dawn, (2) Prime, an early morning service, (3) Tierce at 9 am, (4) Sext at noon, (5) Nones at 3 pm, (6) Vespers at 4 pm, and (7) the bedtime service of Compline.

Coptic calendar. Similar to Orthodox old calendar but with peculiarities.

die dominica. The Lord's Day, Sunday.

dei jovis. The day of Jupiter, Thursday.

die lune. The day of the moon, Monday.

die martis. The day of Mars, Tuesday.

die mercuri. The day of Mercury,Wednesday (Woden's Day).

dei Sabbati. The Sabbath Day, Saturday.

die veneris. The day of Venus, Friday.

dominical letter. Letter A-G denoting the Sundays in successive years and indicating which day of the year the Sunday falls first (ie if the first day of the year is a Sunday then A, if the second day is a Sunday, then B and so on). Used in church calendars and service sheets.

dulia. Festival or service where reverence is paid to angels and saints (as opposed to *latria*).

epact. Described officially as 'The age of the calendar moon diminished by one day on January 1st of the church calendar'.

in crastino. On the morrow, the morning after, or the next day.

intercalary month. Month inserted in a calendar year at various intervals throughout time to make up any difference in the lunar and solar cycles, so bringing them both into line.

in octavis. A week after (seven days after).

in vigia. On the vigil of, the eve of, or the day before.

Julian Calendar. This is the 'Old Style' calendar which is 13 days behind the Orthodox new calendar.

Kalends. Refers to the number of days before the first day of the next month, eg 15th day of Kalends of December would be 17th day of November. The term 'Greek Kalends' is a sarcastic one, meaning *never*, as the Greeks did not have Kalends.

latria. Festival or service where reverence is paid only to God (as opposed to *dulia*).

novennial. Occurring every ninth year.

octave. Eighth day after a church festival (including the day itself).

Orthodox new calendar. Fixed feasts are same as Western calendar but uses old Julian calendar for moveable feasts.

Orthodox old calendar. The Julian Calendar.

post. After.

triodion. Moveable church feasts.

Western calendar. That used by Roman Catholic and Protestant churches.

BIBLIOGRAPHY AND
ACKNOWLEDGEMENTS

Main published reference sources consulted, by title. *(These contain details of other saints not celebrated in the British Isles and Ireland.)*

Abbeys: An Introduction to the religious houses of England and Wales, R. Gilyard Beer, H.M.S.O. 1972

Abbeys, Castles and Ancient Halls of England and Wales, John Timbs, Savill, Edwards and Co, London c1870

All Year Round, Druit, Fynes-Clinton and Rawling, Hawthorn Press, 1995

Amateur Historian magazine (various issues)

Annandale's Concise English Dictionary, Blackie and Son Ltd, Glasgow 1930

Book of Common Prayer, T. Wright and W. Gill, Oxford 1775

Catherine of Aragon, Francesca Claremont, Robert Hale Ltd, London 1939

Christian Calendar, The, Cowie and Gummer, Weidenfield and Nicholson, London 1974

Christian Year, The, J.C.J. Metford, Thames and Hudson, 1991

Church Monthly, London 1901-3

Dictionary of Angels, Gustav Davidson, The Free Press, 1967

Dictionary of Mythology, Fernande Compte, W. and R. Chambers Edinburgh 1991

Evergreen Magazine, A Calendar of Customs and Folklore, Spring 2000

Everyman's Book of Saints, C.P.S. Clarke, A.R. Mowbray and Co Ltd, London 1915

Evil Eye, Frederick Thomas Elsworthy, Julian Press, New York 1958 and 1986

Fire Worship in Britain, T.F.G. Dexter, Watts and Co, London (undated)

Festivals Together, Fitzjohn, Weston and Large, Hawthorn Press, Stroud 1993

Glendalough of the Seven Churches of St Kevin, P.J. Noonan, The People newspapers, Wexford 1936

Gogmagog, T.C. Lethbridge, Routledge and Kegan Paul, 1957

Golden Bough, The, Sir James Frazer, McMillan and Co, 1900

Handbook of British Chronology, Royal Historic Society, 1939

Handbook of Dates, Royal Historic Society, 1939

Harmsworth's Universal Encyclopedia, 1921

History of English Poetry (Vol II), T. Wharton, 1872

History of Witchcraft and Demonology, Montague Summers, Castle Books (U.S.A.), 1992

History of Whitby and of Whitby Abbey, L. Charlton, A. Ward (printers), York 1779

Knights of St John in the British Realm, Sir Edwin King and Sir Harry Luke, Order of St John, 1967

Lives of Saints, Omer Englebert, Barnes and Nobel, New York 1994

Metropolis of the Antique Age: Ephesus, Hüseyin Çimrin, Guney Books Selçuk, Turkey 2000

Pears Shilling Encyclopaedia, A. and F. Pears, London 1913

Standard Dictionary of the English Language, Funk and Wagnalls, London 1901

Story of Danby, Dr R.A. Robinson, privately published ISBN 0 9518352 11

Outlines of English History, George Carter M.A., Relfe Brothers Ltd, London c.1904

Oxford Junior Encyclopedia (Index and Vol I), Oxford Press, London 1957

Quest for the Celtic Key, K. Ralls-Macleod and I. Robinson, Luath Press, Edinburgh 2002

Remaines of Gentilisme and Judaisme, John Aubrey, R.S.S., 1686-87

Rig Veda III, 59, 1

Saints Alive, Enid Broderick Fisher-Fount, Harper Collins, London 1995

Spectator magazine, Vol 2, No. 161, September 1711

Star of Bethlehem Mystery, The, David Hughes, Corgi Books, 1979

Welsh Place Names and their Meanings, Dewi Davies, Cambrian News, Aberystwyth (undated)

Webster's Condensed Dictionary, G. and C. Merriam and Co., U.S.A. 1884

Whitby Lore and Legend, Shaw Jeffrey, Horne and Son, Whitby 1923

Whittaker's Almanack, 108th volume, 1976

Websites consulted:

http://www.byzant.com/festivals/paganfestivals.asp (April 2002)

http://www.crosswinds.net/~daire/names/Saint.html (November 2002)

http://www.geocities.com/Athens/Forum/6946/festivals.html (December 2002)

http://palimpset.stanford.edu/byauth/wooley/calconv.html (December 2002)

http://www.shagtown.com/days (November 2002)

http://www.startinbusiness.co.uk/hols/Saints_celtic.html (November 2002)

http://www.wickham.w-berks.sch.uk/xmas/xmastory.html (December 2002)

Acknowledgements

Thanks are also due to all those people over the years who have provided me with reference sources or pointed me in the direction of records that contained many individual and often obscure festivals, saints' days and other annual events. I am also indebted for the advice and information willingly provided by many aged members of the community. The benefit of their knowledge of the past and its annual festivities has been invaluable.